Captains of Industry
In Their Own Words

JACK DONAHUE

ISBN: 149615553X
ISBN-13: 978-1496155535

DEDICATION

This book is dedicated to the men and women who work to make this country (and this world) move by doing what they do in the white and blue collar worlds. They are different worlds but they make the one we all live on move..

CONTENTS

INTRODUCTION

They say that to get ahead in business, you have to be willing to take heads. You have to be aggressive. You have to have a snazzy suit and a great haircut.

This book contains ten essays on the world of business, written by those who helped make the world of business what it is today.

From P. T. Barnum to Henry Ford and all those in between. We salute those who came, saw a niche that needed filling, and filled it.

Jack Donahue, March 4th, 2014

THE AMERICAN BUSINESS MAN
BY G. K. CHESTERTON

It is a commonplace that men are all agreed in using symbols, and all differ about the meaning of the symbols. It is obvious that a Russian republican might come to identify the eagle as a bird of empire and therefore a bird of prey. But when he ultimately escaped to the land of the free, he might find the same bird on the American coinage figuring as a bird of freedom. Doubtless, he might find many other things to surprise him in the land of the free, and many calculated to make him think that the bird, if not imperial, was at least rather imperious. But I am not discussing those exceptional details here. It is equally obvious that a Russian reactionary might cross the world with a vow of vengeance against the red flag. But that authoritarian might have some difficulties with the authorities, if he shot a man for using the red flag on the railway between Willesden and Clapham Junction.

But, of course, the difficulty about symbols is generally much more subtle than in these simple cases. I have remarked elsewhere that the first thing which a traveller should write about is the thing which he has not read about. It may be a small or secondary thing, but it is a thing that he has seen and not merely expected to see.

I gave the example of the great multitude of wooden houses in America; we might say of wooden towns and wooden cities. But after he has seen such things, his next duty is to see the meaning of them; and here a great deal of

1

complication and controversy is possible. The thing probably does not mean what he first supposes it to mean on the face of it; but even on the face of it, it might mean many different and even opposite things.

For instance, a wooden house might suggest an almost savage solitude; a rude shanty put together by a pioneer in a forest; or it might mean a very recent and rapid solution of the housing problem, conducted cheaply and therefore on a very large scale. A wooden house might suggest the very newest thing in America or one of the very oldest things in England. It might mean a grey ruin at Stratford or a white exhibition at Earl's Court.

It is when we come to this interpretation of international symbols that we make most of the international mistakes. Without the smallest error of detail, I will promise to prove that Oriental women are independent because they wear trousers, or Oriental men subject because they wear skirts. Merely to apply it to this case, I will take the example of two very commonplace and trivial objects of modern life—a walking stick and a fur coat.

As it happened, I travelled about America with two sticks, like a Japanese nobleman with his two swords. I fear the simile is too stately. I bore more resemblance to a cripple with two crutches or a highly ineffectual version of the devil on two sticks. I carried them both because I valued them both, and did not wish to risk losing either of them in my erratic travels. One is a very plain grey stick from the woods of Buckinghamshire, but as I took it with me to Palestine it partakes of the character of a pilgrim's staff. When I can say that I have taken the same stick to Jerusalem and to Chicago, I think the stick and I may both have a rest. The other, which I value even more, was given me by the Knights of Columbus at Yale, and I wish I could think that their chivalric title allowed me to regard it as a sword.

Now, I do not know whether the Americans I met, struck by the fastidious foppery of my dress and appearance, concluded that it is the custom of elegant English dandies to carry two walking sticks. But I do know that it is much less common among Americans than among Englishmen to carry even one. The point, however, is not merely that more sticks are carried by Englishmen than by Americans; it is that the sticks which are carried by Americans stand for something entirely different.

In America a stick is commonly called a cane, and it has about it something of the atmosphere which the poet described as the nice conduct of the clouded cane. It would be an exaggeration to say that when the citizens of the United States see a man carrying a light stick, they deduce that if he does that he does nothing else. But there is about it a faint flavour of luxury and lounging, and most of the energetic citizens of this energetic society avoid it by instinct.

Now, in an Englishman like myself, carrying a stick may imply lounging, but it does not imply luxury, and I can say with some firmness that it does not imply dandyism. In a great many Englishmen it means the very opposite even of lounging. By one of those fantastic paradoxes which are the mystery of nationality, a walking stick often actually means walking. It frequently suggests the very reverse of the beau with his clouded cane; it does not suggest a town type, but rather specially a country type. It rather implies the kind of Englishman who tramps about in lanes and meadows and knocks the tops off thistles. It suggests the sort of man who has carried the stick through his native woods, and perhaps even cut it in his native woods.

There are plenty of these vigorous loungers, no doubt, in the rural parts of America, but the idea of a walking stick would not especially suggest them to Americans; it would not call up such figures like a fairy wand. It would be easy to trace back the difference to many English origins, possibly to aristocratic origins, to the idea of the old squire, a man vigorous and even rustic, but trained to hold a useless staff rather than a useful tool. It might be suggested that American citizens do at least so far love freedom as to like to have their hands free. It might be suggested, on the other hand, that they keep their hands for the handles of many machines. And that the hand on a handle is less free than the hand on a stick or even a tool. But these again are controversial questions and I am only noting a fact.

If an Englishman wished to imagine more or less exactly what the impression is, and how misleading it is, he could find something like a parallel in what he himself feels about a fur coat. When I first found myself among the crowds on the main floor of a New York hotel, my rather exaggerated impression of the luxury of the place was largely produced by the number of men in fur coats, and what we should consider rather ostentatious fur coats, with all the fur outside.

Now an Englishman has a number of atmospheric but largely accidental associations in connection with a fur coat. I will not say that he thinks a man in a fur coat must be a wealthy and wicked man; but I do say that in his own ideal and perfect vision a wealthy and wicked man would wear a fur coat. Thus I had the sensation of standing in a surging mob of American millionaires, or even African millionaires; for the millionaires of Chicago must be like the Knights of the Round Table compared with the millionaires of Johannesburg.

But, as a matter of fact, the man in the fur coat was not even an American millionaire, but simply an American. It did not signify luxury, but rather necessity, and even a harsh and almost heroic necessity. Orson probably wore a fur coat; and he was brought up by bears, but not the bears of Wall Street. Eskimos are generally represented as a furry folk; but they are not necessarily engaged in delicate financial operations, even in the typical and appropriate occupation called freezing out. And if the American is not exactly an arctic traveller rushing from pole to pole, at least he is often literally fleeing from ice to ice. He has to make a very extreme distinction between outdoor and indoor clothing. He has to live in an icehouse outside and a hothouse inside; so hot that he may be said to construct an icehouse inside that. He turns himself into an icehouse and warms himself against the cold until he is warm enough to eat ices. But the point is that the same coat of fur which in England would indicate the sybarite life may here very well indicate the strenuous life; just as the same walking stick which would here suggest a lounger would in England suggest a plodder and almost a pilgrim.

And these two trifles are types which I should like to put, by way of proviso and apology, at the very beginning of any attempt at a record of any impressions of a foreign society. They serve merely to illustrate the most important impression of all, the impression of how false all impressions may be. I suspect that most of the very false impressions have come from the careful record of very true facts. They have come from the fatal power of observing the facts without being able to observe the truth. They came from seeing the symbol with the most vivid clarity and being blind to all that it symbolises. It is as if a man who knew no Greek should imagine that he could read a Greek inscription because he took the Greek R for an English P or the Greek long E for an English H. I do not mention this merely as a criticism on other people's impressions of America, but as a criticism on my own. I wish it to be understood that I am well aware that all my views are subject to this sort of potential criticism, and that even when I am certain of the facts I do not profess to be certain of the deductions.

In this chapter I hope to point out how a misunderstanding of this kind affects the common impression, not altogether unfounded, that the Americans talk about dollars. But for the moment I am merely anxious to avoid a similar misunderstanding when I talk about Americans. About the dogmas of democracy, about the right of a people to its own symbols, whether they be coins or customs, I am convinced, and no longer to be shaken. But about the meaning of those symbols, in silver or other substances, I am always open to correction. That error is the price we pay for the great glory of nationality. And in this sense I am quite ready, at the start, to warn my own readers against my own opinions.

The fact without the truth is futile; indeed the fact without the truth is false. I have already noted that this is especially true touching our observations of a strange country; and it is certainly true touching one small fact which has swelled into a large fable. I mean the fable about America commonly summed up in the phrase about the Almighty Dollar. I do not think the dollar is almighty in America; I fancy many things are mightier, including many ideals and some rather insane ideals. But I think it might be maintained that the dollar has another of the attributes of deity. If it is not omnipotent it is in a sense omnipresent. Whatever Americans think about dollars, it is, I think, relatively true that they talk about dollars. If a mere mechanical record could be taken by the modern machinery of dictaphones and stenography, I do not think it probable that the mere word 'dollars' would occur more often in any given number of American conversations than the mere word 'pounds' or 'shillings' in a similar number of English conversations. And these statistics, like nearly all statistics, would be utterly useless and even fundamentally false. It is as if we should calculate that the word 'elephant' had been mentioned a certain number of times in a particular London street, or so many times more often than the word 'thunderbolt' had been used in Stoke Poges. Doubtless there are statisticians capable of carefully collecting those statistics also; and doubtless there are scientific social reformers capable of legislating on the basis of them. They would probably argue from the elephantine imagery of the London street that such and such a percentage of the householders were megalomaniacs and required medical care and police coercion. And doubtless their calculations, like nearly all such calculations, would leave out the only important point; as that the street was in the immediate neighbourhood of the Zoo, or was yet more happily situated under the benignant shadow of the Elephant and Castle. And in the same way the mechanical calculation about the mention of dollars is entirely useless unless we have some moral understanding of why they are mentioned. It certainly does not mean merely a love of money; and if it did, a love of money may mean a great many very different and even contrary things. The love of money is very different in a peasant or in a pirate, in a miser or in a gambler, in a great financier or in a man doing some practical and productive work. Now this difference in the conversation of American and English business men arises, I think, from certain much deeper things in the American which are generally not understood by the Englishman. It also arises from much deeper things in the Englishman, of which the Englishman is even more ignorant.

To begin with, I fancy that the American, quite apart from any love of money, has a great love of measurement. He will mention the exact size or weight of things, in a way which appears to us as irrelevant. It is as if we were to say that a man came to see us carrying three feet of walking stick and four inches of cigar. It is so in cases that have no possible connection with any avarice or greed for gain. An American will praise the prodigal generosity of some other man in giving up his own estate for the good of the poor. But he will generally say that the philanthropist gave them a 200-acre park, where an Englishman would think it quite sufficient to say that he gave them a park. There is something about this precision which seems suitable to the American atmosphere; to the hard sunlight, and the cloudless skies, and the glittering detail of the architecture and the landscape; just as the vaguer English version is consonant to our mistier and more impressionist scenery. It is also connected perhaps with something more boyish about the younger civilisation; and corresponds to the passionate particularity with which a boy will distinguish the uniforms of regiments, the rigs of ships, or even the colours of tram tickets. It is a certain godlike appetite for things, as distinct from thoughts.

But there is also, of course, a much deeper cause of the difference; and it can easily be deduced by noting the real nature of the difference itself. When two business men in a train are talking about dollars I am not so foolish as to expect them to be talking about the philosophy of St. Thomas Aquinas. But if they were two English business men I should not expect them to be talking about business. Probably it would be about some sport; and most probably some sport in which they themselves never dreamed of indulging. The approximate difference is that the American talks about his work and the Englishman about his holidays. His ideal is not labour but leisure. Like every other national characteristic, this is not primarily a point for praise or blame; in essence it involves neither and in effect it involves both. It is certainly connected with that snobbishness which is the great sin of English society. The Englishman does love to conceive himself as a sort of country gentleman; and his castles in the air are all castles in Scotland rather than in Spain. For, as an ideal, a Scotch castle is as English as a Welsh rarebit or an Irish stew. And if he talks less about money I fear it is sometimes because in one sense he thinks more of it. Money is a mystery in the old and literal sense of something too sacred for speech. Gold is a god; and like the god of some agnostics has no name and is worshipped only in his works. It is true in a sense that the English gentleman wishes to have enough money to be able to forget it. But it may be questioned whether he does entirely forget it. As against this weakness the American has succeeded, at the price of a great deal of crudity and clatter, in making general a very real respect for work. He has partly disenchanted the dangerous glamour of the gentleman, and in that sense has achieved some degree of democracy; which is the most difficult achievement in the world.

On the other hand, there is a good side to the Englishman's day-dream of leisure, and one which the American spirit tends to miss. It may be expressed in the word 'holiday' or still better in the word 'hobby.' The Englishman, in his character of Robin Hood, really has got two strings to his bow. Indeed the Englishman really is well represented by Robin Hood; for there is always something about him that may literally be called outlawed, in the sense of being extra-legal or outside the rules. A Frenchman said of Browning that his centre was not in the middle; and it may be said of many an Englishman that his heart is not where his treasure is. Browning expressed a very English sentiment when he said:—

I like to know a butcher paints,

A baker rhymes for his pursuit,

Candlestick-maker much acquaints

His soul with song, or haply mute

Blows out his brains upon the flute.

Stevenson touched on the same insular sentiment when he said that many men he knew, who were meat-salesmen to the outward eye, might in the life of contemplation sit with the saints. Now the extraordinary achievement of the American meat-salesman is that his poetic enthusiasm can really be for meat sales; not for money but for meat. An American commercial traveller asked me, with a religious fire in his eyes, whether I did not think that salesmanship could be an art. In England there are many salesmen who are sincerely fond of art; but seldom of the art of salesmanship. Art is with them a hobby; a thing of leisure and liberty. That is why the English traveller talks, if not of art, then of sport. That is why the two city men in the London train, if they are not talking about golf, may be talking about gardening. If they are not talking about dollars, or the equivalent of dollars, the reason lies much deeper than any superficial praise or blame touching the desire for wealth. In the English case, at least, it lies very deep in the English spirit. Many of the greatest English things have had this lighter and looser character of a hobby or a holiday experiment. Even a masterpiece has often been a by-product. The works of Shakespeare come out so casually that they can be attributed to the most improbable people; even to Bacon. The sonnets of Shakespeare are picked up afterwards as if out of a wastepaper basket. The immortality of Dr. Johnson does not rest on the written leaves he collected, but entirely on the words he wasted, the words he scattered to the winds. So great a thing as Pickwick is almost a kind of accident; it began as something secondary and grew into something primary and pre-eminent. It began with mere words written to illustrate somebody else's pictures; and swelled like an epic expanded from an epigram. It might almost be said that in the case of Pickwick the author began as the servant of the artist. But, as in the same story of Pickwick, the servant became greater than the master. This incalculable and accidental quality, like all national qualities, has its strength and weakness; but it does represent a certain reserve fund of interests in the Englishman's life; and distinguishes him from the other extreme type, of the millionaire who works till he drops, or who drops because he stops working. It is the great achievement of American civilisation that in that country it really is not cant to talk about the dignity of labour. There is something that might almost be called the sanctity of labour; but it is subject to the profound law that when anything less than the highest becomes a sanctity, it tends also to become a superstition. When the candlestick-maker does not blow out his brains upon the flute there is always a danger that he may blow them out somewhere else, owing to depressed conditions in the candlestick market.

Now certainly one of the first impressions of America, or at any rate of New York, which is by no means the same thing as America, is that of a sort of mob of business men, behaving in many ways in a fashion very different from that of the swarms of London city men who go up every day to the city. They sit about in groups with Red-Indian gravity, as if passing the pipe of peace; though, in fact, most of them are smoking cigars and some of them are eating cigars. The latter strikes me as one of the most peculiar of transatlantic tastes, more peculiar than that of chewing gum. A man will sit for hours consuming a cigar as if it were a sugar-stick; but I should imagine it to be a very disagreeable sugar-stick. Why he attempts to enjoy a cigar without lighting it I do not know; whether it is a more economical way of carrying a mere symbol of commercial conversation; or whether something of the same queer outlandish morality that draws such a distinction between beer and ginger beer draws an equally ethical distinction between touching tobacco and lighting it. For the rest, it would be easy to make a merely external sketch full of things equally strange; for this can always be done in a strange country. I allow for the fact of all foreigners looking alike; but I fancy that all those hard-featured faces, with spectacles and shaven jaws, do look rather alike, because they all like to make their faces hard. And with the mention of their mental attitude we realise the futility of any such external sketch. Unless we can see that these are something more than men smoking cigars and talking about dollars we had much better not see them at all.

It is customary to condemn the American as a materialist because of his worship of success. But indeed this very worship, like any worship, even devil-worship, proves him rather a mystic than a materialist. The Frenchman who retires from business when he has money enough to drink his wine and eat his omelette in peace might much more plausibly be called a materialist by those who do not prefer to call him a man of sense. But Americans do worship success in the abstract, as a sort of ideal vision. They follow success rather than money; they follow money rather than meat and drink. If their national life in one sense is a perpetual game of poker, they are playing excitedly for chips or counters as well as for coins. And by the ultimate test of material enjoyment, like the enjoyment of an omelette, even a coin is itself a counter. The Yankee cannot eat chips as the Frenchman can eat chipped potatoes; but neither can he swallow red cents as the Frenchman swallows red wine. Thus when people say of a Yankee that he worships the dollar, they pay a compliment to his fine spirituality more true and delicate than they imagine. The dollar is an idol because it is an image; but it is an image of success and not of enjoyment.

That this romance is also a religion is shown in the fact that there is a queer sort of morality attached to it. The nearest parallel to it is something like the sense of honour in the old duelling days. There is not a material but a distinctly moral savour about the implied obligation to collect dollars or to collect chips. We hear too much in England of the phrase about 'making good'; for no sensible Englishman favours the needless interlarding of English with scraps of foreign languages. But though it means nothing in English, it means something very particular in American. There is a fine shade of distinction between succeeding and making good, precisely because there must always be a sort of ethical echo in the word good. America does vaguely feel a man making good as something analogous to a man being good or a man doing good. It is connected with his serious self-respect and his sense of being worthy of those he loves. Nor is this curious crude idealism wholly insincere even when it drives him to what some of us would call stealing; any more than the duellist's honour was insincere when it drove him to what some would call murder. A very clever American play which I once saw acted contained a complete working model of this morality. A girl was loyal to, but distressed by, her engagement to a young man on whom there was a sort of cloud of humiliation. The atmosphere was exactly what it would have been in England if he had been accused of cowardice or card-sharping. And there was nothing whatever the matter with the poor young man except that some rotten mine or other in Arizona had not 'made good.' Now in England we should either be below or above that ideal of good. If we were snobs, we should be content to know that he was a gentleman of good connections, perhaps too much accustomed to private means to be expected to be businesslike. If we were somewhat larger-minded people, we should know that he might be as wise as Socrates and as splendid as Bayard and yet be unfitted, perhaps one should say therefore be unfitted, for the dismal and dirty gambling of modern commerce. But whether we were snobbish enough to admire him for being an idler, or chivalrous enough to admire him for being an outlaw, in neither case should we ever really and in our hearts despise him for being a failure. For it is this inner verdict of instinctive idealism that is the point at issue. Of course there is nothing new, or peculiar to the new world, about a man's engagement practically failing through his financial failure. An English girl might easily drop a man because he was poor, or she might stick to him faithfully and defiantly although he was poor. The point is that this girl was faithful but she was not defiant; that is, she was not proud. The whole psychology of the situation was that she shared the weird worldly idealism of her family, and it was wounded as her patriotism would have been wounded if he had betrayed his country. To do them justice, there was nothing to show that they would have had any real respect for a royal duke who had inherited millions; what the simple barbarians wanted was a man who could 'make good.' That the process of making good would probably drag him through the mire of everything bad, that he would make good by bluffing, lying, swindling, and grinding the faces of the poor, did not seem to trouble them in the least. Against this fanaticism there is this shadow of truth even in the fiction of aristocracy; that a gentleman may at least be allowed to be good without being bothered to make it.

Another objection to the phrase about the almighty dollar is that it is an almighty phrase, and therefore an almighty nuisance. I mean that it is made to explain everything, and to explain everything much too well; that is, much too easily. It does not really help people to understand a foreign country; but it gives them the fatal illusion that they do understand it. Dollars stood for America as frogs stood for France; because it was necessary to connect particular foreigners with something, or it would be so easy to confuse a Moor with a Montenegrin or a Russian with a Red Indian. The only cure for this sort of satisfied familiarity is the shock of something really unfamiliar. When people can see nothing at all in American democracy except a Yankee running after a dollar, then the only thing to do is to trip them up as they run after the Yankee, or run away with their notion of the Yankee, by the obstacle of certain odd and obstinate facts that have no relation to that notion. And, as a matter of fact, there are a number of such obstacles to any such generalisation; a number of notable facts that have to be reconciled somehow to our previous notions. It does not matter for this purpose whether the facts are favourable or unfavourable, or whether the qualities are merits or defects; especially as we do not even understand them sufficiently to say which they are. The point is that we are brought to a pause, and compelled to attempt to understand them rather better than we do. We have found the one thing that we did not expect; and therefore the one thing that we cannot explain. And we are moved to an effort, probably an unsuccessful effort, to explain it.

For instance, Americans are very unpunctual. That is the last thing that a critic expects who comes to condemn them for hustling and haggling and vulgar ambition. But it is almost the first fact that strikes the spectator on the spot. The chief difference between the humdrum English business man and the hustling American business man is that the hustling American business man is always late. Of course there is a great deal of difference between coming late and coming too late. But I noticed the fashion first in connection with my own lectures; touching which I could heartily recommend the habit of coming too late. I could easily understand a crowd of commercial Americans not coming to my lectures at all; but there was something odd about their coming in a crowd, and the crowd being expected to turn up some time after the appointed hour. The managers of these lectures (I continue to call them lectures out of courtesy to myself) often explained to me that it was quite useless to begin properly until about half an hour after time. Often people were still coming in three-quarters of an hour or even an hour after time. Not that I objected to that, as some lecturers are said to do; it seemed to me an agreeable break in the monotony; but as a characteristic of a people mostly engaged in practical business, it struck me as curious and interesting. I have grown accustomed to being the most unbusinesslike person in any given company; and it gave me a sort of dizzy exaltation to find I was not the most unpunctual person in that company. I was afterwards told by many Americans that my impression was quite correct; that American unpunctuality was really very prevalent, and extended to much more important things. But at least I was not content to lump this along with all sorts of contrary things that I did not happen to like, and call it America. I am not sure of what it really means, but I rather fancy that though it may seem the very reverse of the hustling, it has the same origin as the hustling. The American is not punctual because he is not punctilious. He is impulsive, and has an impulse to stay as well as an impulse to go. For, after all, punctuality belongs to the same order of ideas as punctuation; and there is no punctuation in telegrams. The order of clocks and set hours which English business has always observed is a good thing in its own way; indeed I think that in a larger sense it is better than the other way. But it is better because it is a protection against hustling, not a promotion of it. In other words, it is better because it is more civilised; as a great Venetian merchant prince clad in cloth of gold was more civilised; or an old English merchant drinking port in an oak-panelled room was more civilised; or a little French shopkeeper shutting up his shop to play dominoes is more civilised. And the reason is that the American has the romance of business and is monomaniac, while the Frenchman has the romance of life and is sane. But the romance of business really is a romance, and the Americans are really romantic about it. And that romance, though it revolves round pork or petrol, is really like a love-affair in this; that it involves not only rushing but also lingering.

The American is too busy to have business habits. He is also too much in earnest to have business rules. If we wish to understand him, we must compare him not with the French shopkeeper when he plays dominoes, but with the same French shopkeeper when he works the guns or mans the trenches as a conscript soldier. Everybody used to the punctilious Prussian standard of uniform and parade has noticed the roughness and apparent laxity of the French soldier, the looseness of his clothes, the unsightliness of his heavy knapsack, in short his inferiority in every detail of the business of war except fighting. There he is much too swift to be smart. He is much too practical to be precise. By a strange illusion which can lift pork-packing almost to the level of patriotism, the American has the same free rhythm in his romance of business. He varies his conduct not to suit the clock but to suit the case. He gives more time to more important and less time to less important things; and he makes up his time-table as he goes along. Suppose he has three appointments; the first, let us say, is some mere trifle of erecting a tower twenty storeys high and exhibiting a sky-sign on the top of it; the second is a business discussion about the possibility of printing advertisements of soft drinks on the table-napkins at a restaurant; the third is attending a conference to decide how the populace can be prevented from using chewing-gum and the manufacturers can still manage to sell it. He will be content merely to glance at the sky-sign as he goes by in a trolley-car or an automobile; he will then settle down to the discussion with his partner about the table-napkins, each speaker indulging in long monologues in turn; a peculiarity of much American conversation. Now if in the middle of one of these monologues, he suddenly thinks that the vacant space of the waiter's shirt-front might also be utilised to advertise the Gee Whiz Ginger Champagne, he will instantly follow up the new idea in all its aspects and possibilities, in an even longer monologue; and will never think of looking at his watch while he is rapturously looking at his waiter. The consequence is that he will come late into the great social movement against chewing-gum, where an Englishman would probably have arrived at the proper hour. But though the Englishman's conduct is more proper, it need not be in all respects more practical. The Englishman's rules are better for the business of life, but not necessarily for the life of business. And it is true that for many of these Americans business is the business of life. It is really also, as I have said, the romance of life. We shall admire or deplore this spirit, accordingly as we are glad to see trade irradiated with so much poetry, or sorry to see so much poetry wasted on trade. But it does make many people happy, like any other hobby; and one is disposed to add that it does fill their imaginations like any other delusion. For the true criticism of all this commercial romance would involve a criticism of this historic phase of commerce. These people are building on the sand, though it shines like gold, and for them like fairy gold; but the world will remember the legend about fairy gold. Half the financial operations they follow deal with things that do not even exist; for in that sense all finance is a fairy tale. Many of them are buying and selling things that do nothing but harm; but it does them good to buy and sell them. The claim of the romantic salesman is better justified than he realises. Business really is romance; for it is not reality.

There is one real advantage that America has over England, largely due to its livelier and more impressionable ideal. America does not think that stupidity is practical. It does not think that ideas are merely destructive things. It does not think that a genius is only a person to be told to go away and blow his brains out; rather it would open all its machinery to the genius and beg him to blow his brains in. It might attempt to use a natural force like Blake or Shelley for very ignoble purposes; it would be quite capable of asking Blake to take his tiger and his golden lions round as a sort of Barnum's Show, or Shelley to hang his stars and haloed clouds among the lights of Broadway. But it would not assume that a natural force is useless, any more than that Niagara is useless. And there is a very definite distinction here touching the intelligence of the trader, whatever we may think of either course touching the intelligence of the artist. It is one thing that Apollo should be employed by Admetus, although he is a god. It is quite another thing that Apollo should always be sacked by Admetus, because he is a god. Now in England, largely owing to the accident of a rivalry and therefore a comparison with France, there arose about the end of the eighteenth century an extraordinary notion that there was some sort of connection between dullness and success. What the Americans call a bonehead became what the English call a hard-headed man. The merchants of London evinced their contempt for the fantastic logicians of Paris by living in a permanent state of terror lest somebody should set the Thames on fire. In this as in much else it is much easier to understand the Americans if we connect them with the French who were their allies than with the English who were their enemies. There are a great many Franco-American resemblances which the practical Anglo-Saxons are of course too hard-headed (or boneheaded) to see. American history is haunted with the shadow of the Plebiscitary President; they have a tradition of classical architecture for public buildings. Their cities are planned upon the squares of Paris and not upon the labyrinth of London. They call their cities Corinth and Syracuse, as the French called their citizens Epaminondas and Timoleon. Their soldiers wore the French kepi; and they make coffee admirably, and do not make tea at all. But of all the French elements in America the most French is this real practicality. They know that at certain times the most businesslike of all qualities is 'l'audace, et encore de l'audace, et toujours de l'audace.' The publisher may induce the poet to do a pot-boiler; but the publisher would cheerfully allow the poet to set the Mississippi on fire, if it would boil his particular pot. It is not so much that Englishmen are stupid as that they are afraid of being clever; and it is not so much that Americans are clever as that they do not try to be any stupider than they are. The fire of French logic has burnt that out of America as it has burnt it out of Europe, and of almost every place except England. This is one of the few points on which English insularity really is a disadvantage. It is the fatal notion that the only sort of commonsense is to be found in compromise, and that the only sort of compromise is to be found in confusion. This must be clearly distinguished from the commonplace about the utilitarian world not rising to the invisible values of genius. Under this philosophy the utilitarian does not see the utility of genius, even when it is quite visible. He does not see it, not because he is a utilitarian, but because he is an idealist whose ideal is dullness. For some time the English aspired to be stupid, prayed and hoped with soaring spiritual ambition to be stupid. But with all their worship of success, they did not succeed in being stupid. The natural talents of a great and traditional nation were always breaking out in spite of them. In spite of the merchants of London, Turner did set the Thames on fire. In spite of our repeatedly explained preference for realism to romance, Europe persisted in resounding with the name of Byron. And just when we had made it perfectly clear to the French that we despised all their flamboyant tricks, that we were a plain prosaic people and there was no fantastic glory or chivalry about us, the very shaft we sent against them shone with the name of Nelson, a shooting and a falling star.

BUSINESS
A SPEECH BY MARK TWAIN

The alumni of Eastman College gave their annual banquet, March 30,1901, at the YMCA Building. Mr. James G. Cannon, of the Fourth National Bank, made the first speech of the evening, after which Mr. Clemens was introduced by Mr. Bailey as the personal friend of Tom Sawyer, who was one of the types of successful business men.

Mr. Cannon has furnished me with texts enough to last as slow a speaker as myself all the rest of the night. I took exception to the introducing of Mr. Cannon as a great financier, as if he were the only great financier present. I am a financier. But my methods are not the same as Mr. Cannon's.

I cannot say that I have turned out the great business man that I thought I was when I began life. But I am comparatively young yet, and may learn. I am rather inclined to believe that what troubled me was that I got the big-head early in the game. I want to explain to you a few points of difference between the principles of business as I see them and those that Mr. Cannon believes in.

He says that the primary rule of business success is loyalty to your employer. That's all right—as a theory. What is the matter with loyalty to yourself? As nearly as I can understand Mr. Cannon's methods, there is one great drawback to them. He wants you to work a great deal. Diligence is a good thing, but taking things easy is much more-restful. My idea is that the employer should be the busy man, and the employee the idle one. The employer should be the worried man, and the employee the happy one. And why not? He gets the salary. My plan is to get another man to do the work for me. In that there's more repose. What I want is repose first, last, and all the time.

Mr. Cannon says that there are three cardinal rules of business success; they are diligence, honesty, and truthfulness. Well, diligence is all right. Let it go as a theory. Honesty is the best policy—when there is money in it. But truthfulness is one of the most dangerous—why, this man is misleading you.

I had an experience to-day with my wife which illustrates this. I was acknowledging a belated invitation to another dinner for this evening, which seemed to have been sent about ten days ago. It only reached me this morning. I was mortified at the discourtesy into which I had been brought by this delay, and wondered what was being thought of me by my hosts. As I had accepted your invitation, of course I had to send regrets to my other friends.

When I started to write this note my wife came up and stood looking over my shoulder. Women always want to know what is going on. Said she "Should not that read in the third person?" I conceded that it should, put aside what I was writing, and commenced over again. That seemed to satisfy her, and so she sat down and let me proceed. I then—finished my first note—and so sent what I intended. I never could have done this if I had let my wife know the truth about it. Here is what I wrote:

TO THE OHIO SOCIETY,—I have at this moment received a most kind invitation (eleven days old) from Mr. Southard, president; and a like one (ten days old) from Mr. Bryant, president of the Press Club. I thank the society cordially for the compliment of these invitations, although I am booked elsewhere and cannot come. But, oh, I should like to know the name of the Lightning Express by which they were forwarded; for I owe a friend a dozen chickens, and I believe it will be cheaper to send eggs instead, and let them develop on the road.
Sincerely yours,
Mark TWAIN.

I want to tell you of some of my experiences in business, and then I will be in a position to lay down one general rule for the guidance of those who want to succeed in business. My first effort was about twenty-five years ago. I took hold of an invention—I don't know now what it was all about, but someone came to me and told me it was a good thing, and that there was lots of money in it. He persuaded me to invest $15,000, and I lived up to my beliefs by engaging a man to develop it. To make a long story short, I sunk $40,000 in it.

Then I took up the publication of a book. I called in a publisher and said to him: "I want you to publish this book along lines which I shall lay down. I am the employer, and you are the employee. I am going to show them some new kinks in the publishing business. And I want you to draw on me for money as you go along," which he did. He drew on me for $56,000. Then I asked him to take the book and call it off. But he refused to do that.

My next venture was with a machine for doing something or other. I knew less about that than I did about the invention. But I sunk $170,000 in the business, and I can't for the life of me recollect what it was the machine was to do.

I was still undismayed. You see, one of the strong points about my business life was that I never gave up. I undertook to publish General Grant's book, and made $140,000 in six months. My axiom is, to succeed in business: avoid my example.

THE DIFFICULT ART OF GETTING
BY JOHN D. ROCKEFELLER

To my father I owe a great debt in that he himself trained me to practical ways. He was engaged in different enterprises; he used to tell me about these things, explaining their significance; and he taught me the principles and methods of business. From early boyhood I kept a little book which I remember I called Ledger A—and this little volume is still preserved—containing my receipts and expenditures as well as an account of the small sums that I was taught to give away regularly.

Naturally, people of modest means lead a closer family life than those who have plenty of servants to do everything for them. I count it a blessing that I was of the former class. When I was seven or eight years old I engaged in my first business enterprise with the assistance of my mother. I owned some turkeys, and she presented me with the curds from the milk to feed them. I took care of the birds myself, [34]and sold them all in business-like fashion. My receipts were all profit, as I had nothing to do with the expense account, and my records were kept as carefully as I knew how.

We thoroughly enjoyed this little business affair, and I can still close my eyes, and distinctly see the gentle and dignified birds walking quietly along the brook and through the woods, cautiously stealing the way to their nests. To this day I enjoy the sight of a flock of turkeys, and never miss an opportunity of studying them.

My mother was a good deal of a disciplinarian, and upheld the standard of the family with a birch switch when it showed a tendency to deteriorate. Once, when I was being punished for some unfortunate doings which had taken place in the village school, I felt called upon to explain after the whipping had begun that I was innocent of the charge.

"Never mind," said my mother, "we have started in on this whipping, and it will do for the next time." This attitude was maintained to its final conclusion in many ways. One night, I remember, we boys could not resist the temptation to go skating in the moonlight, notwithstanding the fact that we had been [35]expressly forbidden to skate at night. Almost before we got fairly started we heard a cry for help, and found a neighbour, who had broken through the ice, was in danger of drowning. By pushing a pole to him we succeeded in fishing him out, and restored him safe and sound to his grateful family. As we were not generally expected to save a man's life every time we skated, my brother William and I felt that there were mitigating circumstances connected with this particular disobedience which might be taken into account in the final judgment, but this idea proved to be erroneous.

STARTING AT WORK

Although the plan had been to send me to college, it seemed best at sixteen that I should leave the high school in which I had nearly completed the course and go into a commercial college in Cleveland for a few months. They taught bookkeeping and some of the fundamental principles of commercial transactions. This training, though it lasted only a few months, was very valuable to me. But how to get a job—that was the question. I tramped the streets for days and weeks, asking merchants and storekeepers if they didn't want a boy; [36]but the offer of my services met with little appreciation. No one wanted a boy, and very few showed any overwhelming anxiety to talk with me on the subject. At last one man on the Cleveland docks told me that I might come back after the noonday meal. I was elated; it now seemed that I might get a start.

I was in a fever of anxiety lest I should lose this one opportunity that I had unearthed. When finally at what seemed to me the time, I presented myself to my would-be employer:

"We will give you a chance," he said, but not a word passed between us about pay. This was September 26, 1855. I joyfully went to work. The name of the firm was Hewitt & Tuttle.

In beginning the work I had some advantages. My father's training, as I have said, was practical, the course at the commercial college had taught me the rudiments of business, and I thus had a groundwork to build upon. I was fortunate, also, in working under the supervision of the bookkeeper, who was a fine disciplinarian, and well disposed toward me.

When January, 1856, arrived, Mr. Tuttle presented me with $50 for my three months' [37]work, which was no doubt all that I was worth, and it was entirely satisfactory.

For the next year, with $25 a month, I kept my position, learning the details and clerical work connected with such a business. It was a wholesale produce commission and forwarding concern, my department being particularly the office duties. Just above me was the bookkeeper for the house, and he received $2,000 a year salary in lieu of his share of the profits of the firm of which he was a member. At the end of the first fiscal year when he left I assumed his clerical and bookkeeping work, for which I received the salary of $500.

As I look back upon this term of business apprenticeship, I can see that its influence was vitally important in its relations to what came after.

To begin with, my work was done in the office of the firm itself. I was almost always present when they talked of their affairs, laid out their plans, and decided upon a course of action. I thus had an advantage over other boys of my age, who were quicker and who could figure and write better than I. The firm conducted a business with so many ramifications that this education was quite extensive. They owned dwelling-houses, ware[38]houses, and buildings which were rented for offices and a variety of uses, and I had to collect the rents. They shipped by rail, canal, and lake. There were many different kinds of negotiations and transactions going on, and with all these I was in close touch.

Thus it happened that my duties were vastly more interesting than those of an office-boy in a large house to-day. I thoroughly enjoyed the work. Gradually the auditing of accounts was left in my hands. All the bills were first passed upon by me, and I took this duty very seriously.

One day, I remember, I was in a neighbour's office, when the local plumber presented himself with a bill about a yard long. This neighbour was one of those very busy men. He was connected with what seemed to me an unlimited number of enterprises. He merely glanced at this tiresome bill, turned to the bookkeeper, and said:

"Please pay this bill."

As I was studying the same plumber's bills in great detail, checking every item, if only for a few cents, and finding it to be greatly to the firm's interest to do so, this casual way of conducting affairs did not appeal to me. I had trained myself to the point of view doubtless held by many young men in business to-day, [39]that my check on a bill was the executive act which released my employer's money from the till and was attended with more responsibility than the spending of my own funds. I made up my mind that such business methods could not succeed.

Passing bills, collecting rents, adjusting claims, and work of this kind brought me in association with a great variety of people. I had to learn how to get on with all these different classes, and still keep the relations between them and the house pleasant. One particular kind of negotiation came to me which took all the skill I could master to bring to a successful end.

We would receive, for example, a shipment of marble from Vermont to Cleveland. This involved handling by railroad, canal, and lake boats. The cost of losses or damage had to be somehow fixed between these three different carriers, and it taxed all the ingenuity of a boy of seventeen to work out this problem to the satisfaction of all concerned, including my employers. But I thought the task no hardship, and so far as I can remember I never had any disagreement of moment with any of these transportation interests. This experience in conducting all sorts of transactions at such an impressionable age, with the [40]helping hand of my superiors to fall back upon in an emergency—was highly interesting to me. It was my first step in learning the principle of negotiation, of which I hope to speak later.

The training that comes from working for some one else, to whom we feel a responsibility, I am sure was of great value to me.

I should estimate that the salaries of that time were far less than half of what is paid for equivalent positions to-day. The next year I was offered a salary of $700, but thought I was worth $800. We had not settled the matter by April, and as a favourable opportunity had presented itself for carrying on the same business on my own account, I resigned my position.

In those days, in Cleveland, everyone knew almost everyone else in town. Among the merchants was a young Englishman named M.B. Clark, perhaps ten years older than I, who wanted to establish a business and was in search of a partner. He had $2,000 to contribute to the firm, and wanted a partner who could furnish an equal amount. This seemed a good opportunity for me. I had saved up $700 or $800, but where to get the rest was a problem.

[41]

I talked the matter over with my father, who told me that he had always intended to give $1,000 to each of his children when they reached twenty-one. He said that if I wished to receive my share at once, instead of waiting, he would advance it to me and I could pay interest upon the sum until I was twenty-one.

"But, John," he added, "the rate is ten."

At that time, 10 per cent. a year interest was a very common rate for such loans. At the banks the rate might not have been quite so high; but of course the financial institutions could not supply all the demands, so there was much private borrowing at high figures. As I needed this money for the partnership, I gladly accepted my father's offer, and so began business as the junior partner of the new firm, which was called Clark & Rockefeller.

It was a great thing to be my own employer. Mentally I swelled with pride—a partner in a firm with $4,000 capital! Mr. Clark attended to the buying and selling, and I took charge of the finance and the books. We at once began to do a large business, dealing in carload lots and cargoes of produce. Naturally we soon needed more money to take care of the increasing trade. There was nothing [42]to do but to attempt to borrow from a bank. But would the bank lend to us?

THE FIRST LOAN

I went to a bank president whom I knew, and who knew me. I remember perfectly how anxious I was to get that loan and to establish myself favourably with the banker. This gentleman was T.P. Handy, a sweet and gentle old man, well known as a high-grade, beautiful character. For fifty years he was interested in young men. He knew me as a boy in the Cleveland schools. I gave him all the particulars of our business, telling him frankly about our affairs—what we wanted to use the money for, etc., etc. I waited for the verdict with almost trembling eagerness.

"How much do you want?" he said.

"Two thousand dollars."

"All right, Mr. Rockefeller, you can have it," he replied. "Just give me your own warehouse receipts; they're good enough for me."

As I left that bank, my elation can hardly be imagined. I held up my head—think of it, a bank had trusted me for $2,000! I felt that I was now a man of importance in the community.

[43]

For long years after the head of this bank was a friend indeed; he loaned me money when I needed it, and I needed it almost all the time, and all the

24

money he had. It was a source of gratification that later I was able to go to him and recommend that he should make a certain investment in Standard Oil stock. He agreed that he would like to do so, but he said that the sum involved was not at the moment available, and so at my suggestion I turned banker for him, and in the end he took out his principal with a very handsome profit. It is a pleasure to testify even at this late date to his great kindness and faith in me.

STICKING TO BUSINESS PRINCIPLES

Mr. Handy trusted me because he believed we would conduct our young business on conservative and proper lines, and I well remember about this time an example of how hard it is sometimes to live up to what one knows is the right business principle. Not long after our concern was started our best customer—that is, the man who made the largest consignments—asked that we should allow him to draw in advance on current shipments before the produce or a bill of lading were actually in hand. We, of course, wished to [44]oblige this important man, but I, as the financial member of the firm, objected, though I feared we should lose his business.

The situation seemed very serious; my partner was impatient with me for refusing to yield, and in this dilemma I decided to go personally to see if I could not induce our customer to relent. I had been unusually fortunate when I came face to face with men in winning their friendship, and my partner's displeasure put me on my mettle. I felt that when I got into touch with this gentleman I could convince him that what he proposed would result in a bad precedent. My reasoning (in my own mind) was logical and convincing. I went to see him, and put forth all the arguments that I had so carefully thought out. But he stormed about, and in the end I had the further humiliation of confessing to my partner that I had failed. I had been able to accomplish absolutely nothing.

Naturally, he was very much disturbed at the possibility of losing our most valued connection, but I insisted and we stuck to our principles and refused to give the shipper the accommodation he had asked. What was our surprise and gratification to find that he con[45]tinued his relations with us as though nothing had happened, and did not again refer to the matter. I learned afterward that an old country banker, named John Gardener, of Norwalk, O., who had much to do with our consignor, was watching this little matter intently, and I have ever since believed that he originated the suggestion to tempt us to do what we stated we did not do as a test, and his story about our firm stand for what we regarded as sound business principles did us great good.

About this time I began to go out and solicit business—a branch of work I had never before attempted. I undertook to visit every person in our part of the country who was in any way connected with the kind of business that we were engaged in, and went pretty well over the states of Ohio and Indiana. I made up my mind that I could do this best by simply introducing our firm, and not pressing for immediate consignments. I told them that I represented Clark & Rockefeller, commission merchants, and that I had no wish to interfere with any connection that they had at present, but if the opportunity offered we should be glad to serve them, etc., etc.

To our great surprise, business came in upon us so fast that we hardly knew how to [46]take care of it, and in the first year our sales amounted to half a million dollars.

Then, and indeed for many years after, it seemed as though there was no end to the money needed to carry on and develop the business. As our successes began to come, I seldom put my head upon the pillow at night without speaking a few words to myself in this wise:

"Now a little success, soon you will fall down, soon you will be overthrown. Because you have got a start, you think you are quite a merchant; look out, or you will lose your head—go steady." These intimate conversations with myself, I am sure, had a great influence on my life. I was afraid I could not stand my prosperity, and tried to teach myself not to get puffed up with any foolish notions.

My loans from my father were many. Our relations on finances were a source of some anxiety to me, and were not quite so humorous as they seem now as I look back at them. Occasionally he would come to me and say that if I needed money in the business he would be able to loan some, and as I always needed capital I was glad indeed to get it, even at 10 per cent. interest. Just at the moment [47]when I required the money most he was apt to say:

"My son, I find I have got to have that money."

"Of course, you shall have it at once," I would answer, but I knew that he was testing me, and that when I paid him, he would hold the money without its earning anything for a little time, and then offer it back later. I confess that this little discipline should have done me good, and perhaps did, but while I concealed it from him, the truth is I was not particularly pleased with his application of tests to discover if my financial ability was equal to such shocks.

INTEREST AT 10 PER CENT.

These experiences with my father remind me that in the early days there was often much discussion as to what should be paid for the use of money. Many people protested that the rate of 10 per cent. was outrageous, and none but a wicked man would exact such a charge. I was accustomed to argue that money was worth what it would bring—no one would pay 10 per cent., or 5 per cent., or 8 per cent. unless the borrower believed that at this rate it was profitable to employ it. As [48]I was always the borrower at that time, I certainly did not argue for paying more than was necessary.

Among the most persistent and heated discussions I ever had were those with the dear old lady who kept the boarding-house where my brother William and I lived when we were away from home at school. I used to greatly enjoy these talks, for she was an able woman and a good talker, and as she charged us only a dollar a week for board and lodging, and fed us well, I certainly was her friend. This was about the usual price for board in the small towns in those days, where the produce was raised almost entirely on the place.

This estimable lady was violently opposed to loaners obtaining high rates of interest, and we had frequent and earnest arguments on the subject. She knew that I was accustomed to make loans for my father, and she was familiar with the rates secured. But all the arguments in the world did not change the rate, and it came down only when the supply of money grew more plentiful.

I have usually found that important alterations in public opinion in regard to business matters have been of slow growth along the line of proved economic theory—very rarely [49]have improvements in these relationships come about through hastily devised legislation.

One can hardly realize how difficult it was to get capital for active business enterprises at that time. In the country farther west much higher rates were paid, which applied usually to personal loans on which a business risk was run, but it shows how different the conditions for young business men were then than now.

A NIMBLE BORROWER

Speaking of borrowing at the banks reminds me of one of the most strenuous financial efforts I ever made. We had to raise the money to accept an offer for a large business. It required many hundreds of thousands of dollars—and in cash—securities would not answer. I received the message at about noon and had to get off on the three-o'clock train. I drove from bank to bank, asking each president or cashier, whomever I could find first, to get ready for me all the funds he could possibly lay hands on. I told them I would be back to get the money later. I rounded up all of our banks in the city, and made a second journey to get the money, and kept going until I secured the necessary amount. With this I was off on the three-o'clock train, and closed the transaction. [50]In these early days I was a good deal of a traveller, visiting our plants, making new connections, seeing people, arranging plans to extend our business—and it often called for very rapid work.

RAISING CHURCH FUNDS

When I was but seventeen or eighteen I was elected as a trustee in the church. It was a mission branch, and occasionally I had to hear members who belonged to the main body speak of the mission as though it were not quite so good as the big mother church. This strengthened our resolve to show them that we could paddle our own canoe.

Our first church was not a very grand affair, and there was a mortgage of $2,000 on it which had been a dispiriting influence for years.

The holder of the mortgage had long demanded that he should be paid, but somehow even the interest was barely kept up, and the creditor finally threatened to sell us out. As it happened, the money had been lent by a deacon in the church, but notwithstanding this fact, he felt that he should have his money, and perhaps he really needed it. Anyhow, he proposed to take such steps as were necessary to get it. The matter came to a head [51]one Sunday morning, when the minister announced from the pulpit that the $2,000 would have to be raised, or we should lose our church building. I therefore found myself at the door of the church as the congregation came and went.

As each member came by I buttonholed him, and got him to promise to give something toward the extinguishing of that debt. I pleaded and urged, and almost threatened. As each one promised, I put his name and the amount down in my little book, and continued to solicit from every possible subscriber.

This campaign for raising the money which started that morning after church, lasted for several months. It was a great undertaking to raise such a sum of money in small amounts ranging from a few cents to the more magnificent promises of gifts to be paid at the rate of twenty-five or fifty cents per week. The plan absorbed me. I contributed what I could, and my first ambition to earn more money was aroused by this and similar undertakings in which I was constantly engaged.

But at last the $2,000 was all in hand and a proud day it was when the debt was extinguished. I hope the members of the mother church were properly humiliated to see how far [52]we had gone beyond their expectations, but I do not now recall that they expressed the surprise that we flattered ourselves they must have felt.

The begging experiences I had at that time were full of interest. I went at the task with pride rather than the reverse, and I continued it until my increasing cares and responsibilities compelled me to resign the actual working out of details to others.

EXCERPTS FROM MY LIFE AND MY WORK
BY HENRY FORD

The Secret of Manufacturing And Serving

Now I am not outlining the career of the Ford Motor Company for any personal reason. I am not saying: "Go thou and do likewise." What I am trying to emphasize is that the ordinary way of doing business is not the best way. I am coming to the point of my entire departure from the ordinary methods. From this point dates the extraordinary success of the company.

We had been fairly following the custom of the trade. Our automobile was less complex than any other. We had no outside money in the concern. But aside from these two points we did not differ materially from the other automobile companies, excepting that we had been somewhat more successful and had rigidly pursued the policy of taking all cash discounts, putting our profits back into the business, and maintaining a large cash balance. We entered cars in all of the races. We advertised and we pushed our sales. Outside of the simplicity of the construction of the car, our main difference in design was that we made no provision for the purely "pleasure car." We were just as much a pleasure car as any other car on the market, but we gave no attention to purely luxury features. We would do special work for a buyer, and I suppose that we would have made a special car at a price. We were a prosperous company. We might easily have sat down and said: "Now we have arrived. Let us hold what we have got."

Indeed, there was some disposition to take this stand. Some of the stockholders were seriously alarmed when our production reached one hundred cars a day. They wanted to do something to stop me from ruining the company, and when I replied to the effect that one hundred cars a day was only a trifle and that I hoped before long to make a thousand a day, they were inexpressibly shocked and I understand seriously contemplated court action. If I had followed the general opinion of my associates I should have kept the business about as it was, put our funds into a fine administration building, tried to make bargains with such competitors as seemed too active, made new designs from time to time to catch the fancy of the public, and generally have passed on into the position of a quiet, respectable citizen with a quiet, respectable business.

The temptation to stop and hang on to what one has is quite natural. I can entirely sympathize with the desire to quit a life of activity and retire to a life of ease. I have never felt the urge myself but I can comprehend what it is— although I think that a man who retires ought entirely to get out of a business. There is a disposition to retire and retain control. It was, however, no part of my plan to do anything of that sort. I regarded our progress merely as an invitation to do more—as an indication that we had reached a place where we might begin to perform a real service. I had been planning every day through these years toward a universal car. The public had given its reactions to the various models. The cars in service, the racing, and the road tests gave excellent guides as to the changes that ought to be made, and even by 1905 I had fairly in mind the specifications of the kind of car I wanted to build. But I lacked the material to give strength without weight. I came across that material almost by accident.

In 1905 I was at a motor race at Palm Beach. There was a big smash-up and a French car was wrecked. We had entered our "Model K"—the high-powered six. I thought the foreign cars had smaller and better parts than we knew anything about. After the wreck I picked up a little valve strip stem. It was very light and very strong. I asked what it was made of. Nobody knew. I gave the stem to my assistant.

"Find out all about this," I told him. "That is the kind of material we ought to have in our cars."

He found eventually that it was a French steel and that there was vanadium in it. We tried every steel maker in America—not one could make vanadium steel. I sent to England for a man who understood how to make the steel commercially. The next thing was to get a plant to turn it out. That was

31

another problem. Vanadium requires 3,000 degrees Fahrenheit. The ordinary furnace could not go beyond 2,700 degrees. I found a small steel company in Canton, Ohio. I offered to guarantee them against loss if they would run a heat for us. They agreed. The first heat was a failure. Very little vanadium remained in the steel. I had them try again, and the second time the steel came through. Until then we had been forced to be satisfied with steel running between 60,000 and 70,000 pounds tensile strength. With vanadium, the strength went up to 170,000 pounds.

Having vanadium in hand I pulled apart our models and tested in detail to determine what kind of steel was best for every part—whether we wanted a hard steel, a tough steel, or an elastic steel. We, for the first time I think, in the history of any large construction, determined scientifically the exact quality of the steel. As a result we then selected twenty different types of steel for the various steel parts. About ten of these were vanadium. Vanadium was used wherever strength and lightness were required. Of course they are not all the same kind of vanadium steel. The other elements vary according to whether the part is to stand hard wear or whether it needs spring—in short, according to what it needs. Before these experiments I believe that not more than four different grades of steel had ever been used in automobile construction. By further experimenting, especially in the direction of heat treating, we have been able still further to increase the strength of the steel and therefore to reduce the weight of the car. In 1910 the French Department of Commerce and Industry took one of our steering spindle connecting rod yokes—selecting it as a vital unit—and tried it against a similar part from what they considered the best French car, and in every test our steel proved the stronger.

The vanadium steel disposed of much of the weight. The other requisites of a universal car I had already worked out and many of them were in practice. The design had to balance. Men die because a part gives out. Machines wreck themselves because some parts are weaker than others. Therefore, a part of the problem in designing a universal car was to have as nearly as possible all parts of equal strength considering their purpose—to put a motor in a one-horse shay. Also it had to be fool proof. This was difficult because a gasoline motor is essentially a delicate instrument and there is a wonderful opportunity for any one who has a mind that way to mess it up. I adopted this slogan:

"When one of my cars breaks down I know I am to blame."

From the day the first motor car appeared on the streets it had to me appeared to be a necessity. It was this knowledge and assurance that led me to build to the one end—a car that would meet the wants of the multitudes. All my efforts were then and still are turned to the production of one car—one model. And, year following year, the pressure was, and still is, to improve and refine and make better, with an increasing reduction in price. The universal car had to have these attributes:

(1) Quality in material to give service in use. Vanadium steel is the strongest, toughest, and most lasting of steels. It forms the foundation and super-structure of the cars. It is the highest quality steel in this respect in the world, regardless of price.

(2) Simplicity in operation—because the masses are not mechanics.

(3) Power in sufficient quantity.

(4) Absolute reliability—because of the varied uses to which the cars would be put and the variety of roads over which they would travel.

(5) Lightness. With the Ford there are only 7.95 pounds to be carried by each cubic inch of piston displacement. This is one of the reasons why Ford cars are "always going," wherever and whenever you see them—through sand and mud, through slush, snow, and water, up hills, across fields and roadless plains.

(6) Control—to hold its speed always in hand, calmly and safely meeting every emergency and contingency either in the crowded streets of the city or on dangerous roads. The planetary transmission of the Ford gave this control and anybody could work it. That is the "why" of the saying: "Anybody can drive a Ford." It can turn around almost anywhere.

(7) The more a motor car weighs, naturally the more fuel and lubricants are used in the driving; the lighter the weight, the lighter the expense of operation. The light weight of the Ford car in its early years was used as an argument against it. Now that is all changed.

The design which I settled upon was called "Model T." The important feature of the new model—which, if it were accepted, as I thought it would be, I intended to make the only model and then start into real production—was its simplicity. There were but four constructional units in the car—the power plant, the frame, the front axle, and the rear axle. All of these were easily accessible and they were designed so that no special skill would be required for their repair or replacement. I believed then, although I said very little about it because of the novelty of the idea, that it ought to be possible to have parts so simple and so inexpensive that the menace of expensive hand repair work would be entirely eliminated. The parts could be made so cheaply that it would be less expensive to buy new ones than to have old ones repaired. They could be carried in hardware shops just as nails or bolts are carried. I thought that it was up to me as the designer to make the car so completely simple that no one could fail to understand it.

That works both ways and applies to everything. The less complex an article, the easier it is to make, the cheaper it may be sold, and therefore the greater number may be sold.

It is not necessary to go into the technical details of the construction but perhaps this is as good a place as any to review the various models, because "Model T" was the last of the models and the policy which it brought about took this business out of the ordinary line of business. Application of the same idea would take any business out of the ordinary run.

I designed eight models in all before "Model T." They were: "Model A," "Model B," "Model C," "Model F," "Model N," "Model R," "Model S," and "Model K." Of these, Models "A," "C," and "F" had two-cylinder opposed horizontal motors. In "Model A" the motor was at the rear of the driver's seat. In all of the other models it was in a hood in front. Models "B," "N," "R," and "S" had motors of the four-cylinder vertical type. "Model K" had six cylinders. "Model A" developed eight horsepower. "Model B" developed twenty-four horsepower with a 4-1/2-inch cylinder and a 5-inch stroke. The highest horsepower was in "Model K," the six-cylinder car, which developed forty horsepower. The largest cylinders were those of "Model B." The smallest were in Models "N," "R," and "S" which were 3-3/4 inches in diameter with a 3-3/8-inch stroke. "Model T" has a 3-3/4-inch cylinder with a 4-inch stroke. The ignition was by dry batteries in all excepting "Model B," which had storage batteries, and in "Model K" which had both battery and magneto. In the present model, the magneto is a part of the power plant and is built in. The clutch in the first four models was of the cone type; in the last four and in the present model, of the multiple disc type. The transmission in all of the cars has been planetary. "Model A" had a chain drive. "Model B" had a shaft drive. The next two models had chain drives. Since then all of the cars have had shaft drives. "Model A" had a 72-inch wheel base. Model "B," which was an extremely good car, had 92 inches. "Model K" had 120 inches. "Model C" had 78 inches. The others had 84 inches, and the present car has 100 inches. In the first five models all of the equipment was extra. The next three were sold with a partial equipment. The present car is sold with full equipment. Model "A" weighed 1,250 pounds. The lightest cars were Models "N" and "R." They weighed 1,050 pounds, but they were both runabouts. The heaviest car was the six-cylinder, which weighed 2,000 pounds. The present car weighs 1,200 lbs.

The "Model T" had practically no features which were not contained in some one or other of the previous models. Every detail had been fully tested in practice. There was no guessing as to whether or not it would be a successful model. It had to be. There was no way it could escape being so, for it had not been made in a day. It contained all that I was then able to put into a motor car plus the material, which for the first time I was able to obtain. We put out "Model T" for the season 1908-1909.

The company was then five years old. The original factory space had been .28 acre. We had employed an average of 311 people in the first year, built 1,708 cars, and had one branch house. In 1908, the factory space had increased to 2.65 acres and we owned the building. The average number of employees had increased to 1,908. We built 6,181 cars and had fourteen branch houses. It was a prosperous business.

During the season 1908-1909 we continued to make Models "R" and "S," four-cylinder runabouts and roadsters, the models that had previously been so successful, and which sold at $700 and $750. But "Model T" swept them right out. We sold 10,607 cars—a larger number than any manufacturer had ever sold. The price for the touring car was $850. On the same chassis we mounted a town car at $1,000, a roadster at $825, a coupe at $950, and a landaulet at $950.

This season demonstrated conclusively to me that it was time to put the new policy in force. The salesmen, before I had announced the policy, were spurred by the great sales to think that even greater sales might be had if only we had more models. It is strange how, just as soon as an article becomes successful, somebody starts to think that it would be more successful if only it were different. There is a tendency to keep monkeying with styles and to spoil a good thing by changing it. The salesmen were insistent on increasing the line. They listened to the 5 per cent., the special customers who could say what they wanted, and forgot all about the 95 per cent. who just bought without making any fuss. No business can improve unless it pays the closest possible attention to complaints and suggestions. If there is any defect in service then that must be instantly and rigorously investigated, but when the suggestion is only as to style, one has to make sure whether it is not merely a personal whim that is being voiced. Salesmen always want to cater to whims instead of acquiring sufficient knowledge of their product to be able to explain to the customer with the whim that what they have will satisfy his every requirement—that is, of course, provided what they have does satisfy these requirements.

Therefore in 1909 I announced one morning, without any previous warning, that in the future we were going to build only one model, that the model was going to be "Model T," and that the chassis would be exactly the same for all cars, and I remarked:

"Any customer can have a car painted any colour that he wants so long as it is black."

I cannot say that any one agreed with me. The selling people could not of course see the advantages that a single model would bring about in production. More than that, they did not particularly care. They thought that our production was good enough as it was and there was a very decided opinion that lowering the sales price would hurt sales, that the people who wanted quality would be driven away and that there would be none to replace them. There was very little conception of the motor industry. A motor car was still regarded as something in the way of a luxury. The manufacturers did a good deal to spread this idea. Some clever persons invented the name "pleasure car" and the advertising emphasized the pleasure features. The sales people had ground for their objections and particularly when I made the following announcement:

"I will build a motor car for the great multitude. It will be large enough for the family but small enough for the individual to run and care for. It will be constructed of the best materials, by the best men to be hired, after the simplest designs that modern engineering can devise. But it will be so low in price that no man making a good salary will be unable to own one—and enjoy with his family the blessing of hours of pleasure in God's great open spaces."

This announcement was received not without pleasure. The general comment was:

"If Ford does that he will be out of business in six months."

The impression was that a good car could not be built at a low price, and that, anyhow, there was no use in building a low-priced car because only wealthy people were in the market for cars. The 1908-1909 sales of more than ten thousand cars had convinced me that we needed a new factory. We already had a big modern factory—the Piquette Street plant. It was as good as, perhaps a little better than, any automobile factory in the country. But I did not see how it was going to care for the sales and production that were inevitable. So I bought sixty acres at Highland Park, which was then considered away out in the country from Detroit. The amount of ground bought and the plans for a bigger factory than the world has ever seen were opposed. The question was already being asked:

"How soon will Ford blow up?"

Nobody knows how many thousand times it has been asked since. It is asked only because of the failure to grasp that a principle rather than an individual is at work, and the principle is so simple that it seems mysterious.

For 1909-1910, in order to pay for the new land and buildings, I slightly raised the prices. This is perfectly justifiable and results in a benefit, not an injury, to the purchaser. I did exactly the same thing a few years ago—or rather, in that case I did not lower the price as is my annual custom, in order to build the River Rouge plant. The extra money might in each case have been had by borrowing, but then we should have had a continuing charge upon the business and all subsequent cars would have had to bear this charge. The price of all the models was increased $100, with the exception of the roadster, which was increased only $75 and of the landaulet and town car, which were increased $150 and $200 respectively. We sold 18,664 cars, and then for 1910-1911, with the new facilities, I cut the touring car from $950 to $780 and we sold 34,528 cars. That is the beginning of the steady reduction in the price of the cars in the face of ever-increasing cost of materials and ever-higher wages.

Contrast the year 1908 with the year 1911. The factory space increased from 2.65 to 32 acres. The average number of employees from 1,908 to 4,110, and the cars built from a little over six thousand to nearly thirty-five thousand. You will note that men were not employed in proportion to the output.

We were, almost overnight it seems, in great production. How did all this come about?

Simply through the application of an inevitable principle. By the application of intelligently directed power and machinery. In a little dark shop on a side street an old man had laboured for years making axe handles. Out of seasoned hickory he fashioned them, with the help of a draw shave, a chisel, and a supply of sandpaper. Carefully was each handle weighed and balanced. No two of them were alike. The curve must exactly fit the hand and must conform to the grain of the wood. From dawn until dark the old man laboured. His average product was eight handles a week, for which he received a dollar and a half each. And often some of these were unsaleable—because the balance was not true.

To-day you can buy a better axe handle, made by machinery, for a few cents. And you need not worry about the balance. They are all alike—and every one is perfect. Modern methods applied in a big way have not only brought the cost of axe handles down to a fraction of their former cost— but they have immensely improved the product.

It was the application of these same methods to the making of the Ford car that at the very start lowered the price and heightened the quality. We just developed an idea. The nucleus of a business may be an idea. That is, an inventor or a thoughtful workman works out a new and better way to serve some established human need; the idea commends itself, and people want to avail themselves of it. In this way a single individual may prove, through his idea or discovery, the nucleus of a business. But the creation of the body and bulk of that business is shared by everyone who has anything to do with it. No manufacturer can say: "I built this business"—if he has required the help of thousands of men in building it. It is a joint production. Everyone employed in it has contributed something to it. By working and producing they make it possible for the purchasing world to keep coming to that business for the type of service it provides, and thus they help establish a custom, a trade, a habit which supplies them with a livelihood. That is the way our company grew and just how I shall start explaining in the next chapter.

In the meantime, the company had become world-wide. We had branches in London and in Australia. We were shipping to every part of the world, and in England particularly we were beginning to be as well known as in America. The introduction of the car in England was somewhat difficult on account of the failure of the American bicycle. Because the American bicycle had not been suited to English uses it was taken for granted and made a point of by the distributors that no American vehicle could appeal to the British market. Two "Model A's" found their way to England in 1903. The newspapers refused to notice them. The automobile agents refused to take the slightest interest. It was rumoured that the principal components of its manufacture were string and hoop wire and that a buyer would be lucky if it held together for a fortnight! In the first year about a dozen cars in all were used; the second was only a little better. And I may say as to the reliability of that "Model A" that most of them after nearly twenty years are still in some kind of service in England.

In 1905 our agent entered a "Model C" in the Scottish Reliability Trials. In those days reliability runs were more popular in England than motor races. Perhaps there was no inkling that after all an automobile was not merely a toy. The Scottish Trials was over eight hundred miles of hilly, heavy roads. The Ford came through with only one involuntary stop against it. That started the Ford sales in England. In that same year Ford taxicabs were placed in London for the first time. In the next several years the sales began to pick up. The cars went into every endurance and reliability test and won every one of them. The Brighton dealer had ten Fords driven over the South Downs for two days in a kind of steeplechase and every one of them came through. As a result six hundred cars were sold that year. In 1911 Henry Alexander drove a "Model T" to the top of Ben Nevis, 4,600 feet. That year 14,060 cars were sold in England, and it has never since been necessary to stage any kind of a stunt. We eventually opened our own factory at Manchester; at first it was purely an assembling plant. But as the years have gone by we have progressively made more and more of the car.

How Cheaply Can Things Be Made

No one will deny that if prices are sufficiently low, buyers will always be found, no matter what are supposed to be the business conditions. That is one of the elemental facts of business. Sometimes raw materials will not move, no matter how low the price. We have seen something of that during the last year, but that is because the manufacturers and the distributors were trying to dispose of high-cost stocks before making new engagements. The markets were stagnant, but not "saturated" with goods. What is called a "saturated" market is only one in which the prices are above the purchasing power.

Unduly high prices are always a sign of unsound business, because they are always due to some abnormal condition. A healthy patient has a normal temperature; a healthy market has normal prices. High prices come about commonly by reason of speculation following the report of a shortage. Although there is never a shortage in everything, a shortage in just a few important commodities, or even in one, serves to start speculation. Or again, goods may not be short at all. An inflation of currency or credit will cause a quick bulge in apparent buying power and the consequent opportunity to speculate. There may be a combination of actual shortages and a currency inflation—as frequently happens during war. But in any condition of unduly high prices, no matter what the real cause, the people pay the high prices because they think there is going to be a shortage. They may buy bread ahead of their own needs, so as not to be left later in the lurch, or they may buy in the hope of reselling at a profit. When there was talk of a sugar shortage, housewives who had never in their lives bought more than ten pounds of sugar at once tried to get stocks of one hundred or two hundred pounds, and while they were doing this, speculators were buying sugar to store in warehouses. Nearly all our war shortages were caused by speculation or buying ahead of need.

No matter how short the supply of an article is supposed to be, no matter if the Government takes control and seizes every ounce of that article, a man who is willing to pay the money can always get whatever supply he is willing to pay for. No one ever knows actually how great or how small is the national stock of any commodity. The very best figures are not more than guesses; estimates of the world's stock of a commodity are still wilder. We may think we know how much of a commodity is produced on a certain day or in a certain month, but that does not tell us how much will be produced the next day or the next month. Likewise we do not know how much is consumed. By spending a great deal of money we might, in the course of time, get at fairly accurate figures on how much of a particular commodity was consumed over a period, but by the time those figures were compiled they would be utterly useless except for historical purposes, because in the next period the consumption might be double or half as much. People do not stay put. That is the trouble with all the framers of Socialistic and Communistic, and of all other plans for the ideal regulation of society. They all presume that people will stay put. The reactionary has the same idea. He insists that everyone ought to stay put. Nobody does, and for that I am thankful.

Consumption varies according to the price and the quality, and nobody knows or can figure out what future consumption will amount to, because every time a price is lowered a new stratum of buying power is reached. Everyone knows that, but many refuse to recognize it by their acts. When a storekeeper buys goods at a wrong price and finds they will not move, he reduces the price by degrees until they do move. If he is wise, instead of nibbling at the price and encouraging in his customers the hope of even lower prices, he takes a great big bite out of the price and gets the stuff out of his place. Everyone takes a loss on some proposition of sales. The common hope is that after the loss there may be a big profit to make up for the loss. That is usually a delusion. The profit out of which the loss has to be taken must be found in the business preceding the cut. Any one who was foolish enough to regard the high profits of the boom period as permanent profits got into financial trouble when the drop came. However, there is a belief, and a very strong one, that business consists of a series of profits and losses, and good business is one in which the profits exceed the losses. Therefore some men reason that the best price to sell at is the highest price which may be had. That is supposed to be good business practice. Is it? We have not found it so.

We have found in buying materials that it is not worth while to buy for other than immediate needs. We buy only enough to fit into the plan of production, taking into consideration the state of transportation at the time. If transportation were perfect and an even flow of materials could be assured, it would not be necessary to carry any stock whatsoever. The carloads of raw materials would arrive on schedule and in the planned order and amounts, and go from the railway cars into production. That would save a great deal of money, for it would give a very rapid turnover and thus decrease the amount of money tied up in materials. With bad transportation one has to carry larger stocks. At the time of revaluing the inventory in 1921 the stock was unduly high because transportation had been so bad. But we learned long ago never to buy ahead for speculative purposes. When prices are going up it is considered good business to buy far ahead, and when prices are up to buy as little as possible. It needs no argument to demonstrate that, if you buy materials at ten cents a pound and the material goes later to twenty cents a pound you will have a distinct advantage over the man who is compelled to buy at twenty cents. But we have found that thus buying ahead does not pay. It is entering into a guessing contest. It is not business. If a man buys a large stock at ten cents, he is in a fine position as long as the other man is paying twenty cents. Then he later gets a chance to buy more of the material at twenty cents, and it seems to be a good buy because everything points to the price going to thirty cents. Having great satisfaction in his previous judgment, on which he made money, he of course makes the new purchase. Then the price drops and he is just where he started. We have carefully figured, over the years, that buying ahead of requirements does not pay—that the gains on one purchase will be offset by the losses on another, and in the end we have gone to a great deal of trouble without any corresponding benefit. Therefore in our buying we simply get the best price we can for the quantity that we require. We do not buy less if the price be high and we do not buy more if the price be low. We carefully avoid bargain lots in excess of requirements. It was not easy to reach that decision. But in the end speculation will kill any manufacturer. Give him a couple of good purchases on which he makes money and before long he will be thinking more about making money out of buying and selling than out of his legitimate business, and he will smash. The only way to keep out of trouble is to buy what one needs—no more and no less. That course removes one hazard from business.

This buying experience is given at length because it explains our selling policy. Instead of giving attention to competitors or to demand, our prices are based on an estimate of what the largest possible number of people will want to pay, or can pay, for what we have to sell. And what has resulted from that policy is best evidenced by comparing the price of the touring car and the production.

> YEAR PRICE PRODUCTION 1909-10 $950 18,664 cars 1910-11 $780 34,528 " 1911-12 $690 78,440 " 1912-13 $600 168,220 " 1913-14 $550 248,307 " 1914-15 $490 308,213 " 1915-16 $440 533,921 " 1916-17 $360 785,432 " 1917-18 $450 706,584 " 1918-19 $525 533,706 " (The above two years were war years and the factory was in war work). 1919-20 $575 to $440 996,660 " 1920-21 $440 to $355 1,250,000 "

The high prices of 1921 were, considering the financial inflation, not really high. At the time of writing the price is $497. These prices are actually lower than they appear to be, because improvements in quality are being steadily made. We study every car in order to discover if it has features that might be developed and adapted. If any one has anything better than we have we want to know it, and for that reason we buy one of every new car that comes out. Usually the car is used for a while, put through a road test, taken apart, and studied as to how and of what everything is made. Scattered about Dearborn there is probably one of nearly every make of car on earth. Every little while when we buy a new car it gets into the newspapers and somebody remarks that Ford doesn't use the Ford. Last year we ordered a big Lanchester—which is supposed to be the best car in England. It lay in our Long Island factory for several months and then I decided to drive it to Detroit. There were several of us and we had a little caravan—the Lanchester, a Packard, and a Ford or two. I happened to be riding in the Lanchester passing through a New York town and when the reporters came up they wanted to know right away why I was not riding in a Ford.

"Well, you see, it is this way," I answered. "I am on a vacation now; I am in no hurry, we do not care much when we get home. That is the reason I am not in the Ford."

You know, we also have a line of "Ford stories"!

Our policy is to reduce the price, extend the operations, and improve the article. You will notice that the reduction of price comes first. We have never considered any costs as fixed. Therefore we first reduce the price to a point where we believe more sales will result. Then we go ahead and try to make the price. We do not bother about the costs. The new price forces the costs down. The more usual way is to take the costs and then determine the price, and although that method may be scientific in the narrow sense, it is not scientific in the broad sense, because what earthly use is it to know the cost if it tells you you cannot manufacture at a price at which the article can be sold? But more to the point is the fact that, although one may calculate what a cost is, and of course all of our costs are carefully calculated, no one knows what a cost ought to be. One of the ways of discovering what a cost ought to be is to name a price so low as to force everybody in the place to the highest point of efficiency. The low price makes everybody dig for profits. We make more discoveries concerning manufacturing and selling under this forced method than by any method of leisurely investigation.

The payment of high wages fortunately contributes to the low costs because the men become steadily more efficient on account of being relieved of outside worries. The payment of five dollars a day for an eight-hour day was one of the finest cost-cutting moves we ever made, and the six-dollar day wage is cheaper than the five. How far this will go, we do not know.

We have always made a profit at the prices we have fixed and, just as we have no idea how high wages will go, we also have no idea how low prices will go, but there is no particular use in bothering on that point. The tractor, for instance, was first sold for $750, then at $850, then at $625, and the other day we cut it 37 per cent, to $395. The tractor is not made in connection with the automobiles. No plant is large enough to make two articles. A shop has to be devoted to exactly one product in order to get the real economies.

For most purposes a man with a machine is better than a man without a machine. By the ordering of design of product and of manufacturing process we are able to provide that kind of a machine which most multiplies the power of the hand, and therefore we give to that man a larger role of service, which means that he is entitled to a larger share of comfort.

Keeping that principle in mind we can attack waste with a definite objective. We will not put into our establishment anything that is useless. We will not put up elaborate buildings as monuments to our success. The interest on the investment and the cost of their upkeep only serve to add uselessly to the cost of what is produced—so these monuments of success are apt to end as tombs. A great administration building may be necessary. In me it arouses a suspicion that perhaps there is too much administration. We have never found a need for elaborate administration and would prefer to be advertised by our product than by where we make our product.

The standardization that effects large economies for the consumer results in profits of such gross magnitude to the producer that he can scarcely know what to do with his money. But his effort must be sincere, painstaking, and fearless. Cutting out a half-a-dozen models is not standardizing. It may be, and usually is, only the limiting of business, for if one is selling on the ordinary basis of profit—that is, on the basis of taking as much money away from the consumer as he will give up—then surely the consumer ought to have a wide range of choice.

Standardization, then, is the final stage of the process. We start with consumer, work back through the design, and finally arrive at manufacturing. The manufacturing becomes a means to the end of service.

It is important to bear this order in mind. As yet, the order is not thoroughly understood. The price relation is not understood. The notion persists that prices ought to be kept up. On the contrary, good business—large consumption—depends on their going down.

And here is another point. The service must be the best you can give. It is considered good manufacturing practice, and not bad ethics, occasionally to change designs so that old models will become obsolete and new ones will have to be bought either because repair parts for the old cannot be had, or because the new model offers a new sales argument which can be used to persuade a consumer to scrap what he has and buy something new. We have been told that this is good business, that it is clever business, that the object of business ought to be to get people to buy frequently and that it is bad business to try to make anything that will last forever, because when once a man is sold he will not buy again.

Our principle of business is precisely to the contrary. We cannot conceive how to serve the consumer unless we make for him something that, as far as we can provide, will last forever. We want to construct some kind of a machine that will last forever. It does not please us to have a buyer's car wear out or become obsolete. We want the man who buys one of our products never to have to buy another. We never make an improvement that renders any previous model obsolete. The parts of a specific model are not only interchangeable with all other cars of that model, but they are interchangeable with similar parts on all the cars that we have turned out. You can take a car of ten years ago and, buying to-day's parts, make it with very little expense into a car of to-day. Having these objectives the costs always come down under pressure. And since we have the firm policy of steady price reduction, there is always pressure. Sometimes it is just harder!

Take a few more instances of saving. The sweepings net six hundred thousand dollars a year. Experiments are constantly going on in the utilization of scrap. In one of the stamping operations six-inch circles of sheet metal are cut out. These formerly went into scrap. The waste worried the men. They worked to find uses for the discs. They found that the plates were just the right size and shape to stamp into radiator caps but the metal was not thick enough. They tried a double thickness of plates, with the result that they made a cap which tests proved to be stronger than one made out of a single sheet of metal. We get 150,000 of those discs a day. We have now found a use for about 20,000 a day and expect to find further uses for the remainder. We saved about ten dollars each by making transmissions instead of buying them. We experimented with bolts and produced a special bolt made on what is called an "upsetting machine" with a rolled thread that was stronger than any bolt we could buy, although in its making was used only about one third of the material that the outside manufacturers used. The saving on one style of bolt alone amounted to half a million dollars a year. We used to assemble our cars at Detroit, and although by special packing we managed to get five or six into a freight car, we needed many hundreds of freight cars a day. Trains were moving in and out all the time. Once a thousand freight cars were packed in a single day. A certain amount of congestion was inevitable. It is very expensive to knock down machines and crate them so that they cannot be injured in transit—to say nothing of the transportation charges. Now, we assemble only three or four hundred cars a day at Detroit—just enough for local needs. We now ship the parts to our assembling stations all over the United States and in fact pretty much all over the world, and the machines are put together there. Wherever it is possible for a branch to make a part more cheaply than we can make it in Detroit and ship it to them, then the branch makes the part.

The plant at Manchester, England, is making nearly an entire car. The tractor plant at Cork, Ireland, is making almost a complete tractor. This is an enormous saving of expense and is only an indication of what may be done throughout industry generally, when each part of a composite article is made at the exact point where it may be made most economically. We are constantly experimenting with every material that enters into the car. We cut most of our own lumber from our own forests. We are experimenting in the manufacture of artificial leather because we use about forty thousand yards of artificial leather a day. A penny here and a penny there runs into large amounts in the course of a year.

The greatest development of all, however, is the River Rouge plant, which, when it is running to its full capacity, will cut deeply and in many directions into the price of everything we make. The whole tractor plant is now there. This plant is located on the river on the outskirts of Detroit and the property covers six hundred and sixty-five acres—enough for future development. It has a large slip and a turning basin capable of accommodating any lake steamship; a short-cut canal and some dredging will give a direct lake connection by way of the Detroit River. We use a great deal of coal. This coal comes directly from our mines over the Detroit, Toledo and Ironton Railway, which we control, to the Highland Park plant and the River Rouge plant. Part of it goes for steam purposes. Another part goes to the by-product coke ovens which we have established at the River Rouge plant. Coke moves on from the ovens by mechanical transmission to the blast furnaces. The low volatile gases from the blast furnaces are piped to the power plant boilers where they are joined by the sawdust and the shavings from the body plant—the making of all our bodies has been shifted to this plant—and in addition the coke "breeze" (the dust in the making of coke) is now also being utilized for stoking. The steam power plant is thus fired almost exclusively from what would otherwise be waste products. Immense steam turbines directly coupled with dynamos transform this power into electricity, and all of the machinery in the tractor and the body plants is run by individual motors from this electricity. In the course of time it is expected that there will be sufficient electricity to run practically the whole Highland Park plant, and we shall then have cut out our coal bill.

Among the by-products of the coke ovens is a gas. It is piped both to the Rouge and Highland Park plants where it is used for heat-treat purposes, for the enamelling ovens, for the car ovens, and the like. We formerly had to buy this gas. The ammonium sulphate is used for fertilizer. The benzol is a motor fuel. The small sizes of coke, not suitable for the blast furnaces, are sold to the employees—delivered free into their homes at much less than the ordinary market price. The large-sized coke goes to the blast furnaces. There is no manual handling. We run the melted iron directly from the blast furnaces into great ladles. These ladles travel into the shops and the iron is poured directly into the moulds without another heating. We thus not only get a uniform quality of iron according to our own specifications and directly under our control, but we save a melting of pig iron and in fact cut out a whole process in manufacturing as well as making available all our own scrap.

What all this will amount to in point of savings we do not know—that is, we do not know how great will be the saving, because the plant has not been running long enough to give more than an indication of what is ahead, and we save in so many directions—in transportation, in the generation of our power, in the generation of gas, in the expense in casting, and then over and above that is the revenue from the by-products and from the smaller sizes of coke. The investment to accomplish these objects to date amounts to something over forty million dollars.

How far we shall thus reach back to sources depends entirely on circumstances. Nobody anywhere can really do more than guess about the future costs of production. It is wiser to recognize that the future holds more than the past—that every day holds within it an improvement on the methods of the day before.

But how about production? If every necessary of life were produced so cheaply and in such quantities, would not the world shortly be surfeited with goods? Will there not come a point when, regardless of price, people simply will not want anything more than what they already have? And if in the process of manufacturing fewer and fewer men are used, what is going to become of these men—how are they going to find jobs and live?

Take the second point first. We mentioned many machines and many methods that displaced great numbers of men and then someone asks:

"Yes, that is a very fine idea from the standpoint of the proprietor, but how about these poor fellows whose jobs are taken away from them?"

The question is entirely reasonable, but it is a little curious that it should be asked. For when were men ever really put out of work by the bettering of industrial processes? The stage-coach drivers lost their jobs with the coming of the railways. Should we have prohibited the railways and kept the stage-coach drivers? Were there more men working with the stage-coaches than are working on the railways? Should we have prevented the taxicab because its coming took the bread out of the mouths of the horse-cab drivers? How does the number of taxicabs compare with the number of horse-cabs when the latter were in their prime? The coming of shoe machinery closed most of the shops of those who made shoes by hand. When shoes were made by hand, only the very well-to-do could own more than a single pair of shoes, and most working people went barefooted in summer. Now, hardly any one has only one pair of shoes, and shoe making is a great industry. No, every time you can so arrange that one man will do the work of two, you so add to the wealth of the country that there will be a new and better job for the man who is displaced. If whole industries changed overnight, then disposing of the surplus men would be a problem, but these changes do not occur as rapidly as that. They come gradually. In our own experience a new place always opens for a man as soon as better processes have taken his old job. And what happens in my shops happens everywhere in industry. There are many times more men to-day employed in the steel industries than there were in the days when every operation was by hand. It has to be so. It always is so and always will be so. And if any man cannot see it, it is because he will not look beyond his own nose.

Now as to saturation. We are continually asked:

"When will you get to the point of overproduction? When will there be more cars than people to use them?"

We believe it is possible some day to reach the point where all goods are produced so cheaply and in such quantities that overproduction will be a reality. But as far as we are concerned, we do not look forward to that condition with fear—we look forward to it with great satisfaction. Nothing could be more splendid than a world in which everybody has all that he wants. Our fear is that this condition will be too long postponed. As to our own products, that condition is very far away. We do not know how many motor cars a family will desire to use of the particular kind that we make. We know that, as the price has come down, the farmer, who at first used one car (and it must be remembered that it is not so very long ago that the farm market for motor cars was absolutely unknown—the limit of sales was at that time fixed by all the wise statistical sharps at somewhere near the number of millionaires in the country) now often uses two, and also he buys a truck. Perhaps, instead of sending workmen out to scattered jobs in a single car, it will be cheaper to send each worker out in a car of his own. That is happening with salesmen. The public finds its own consumptive needs with unerring accuracy, and since we no longer make motor cars or tractors, but merely the parts which when assembled become motor cars and tractors, the facilities as now provided would hardly be sufficient to provide replacements for ten million cars. And it would be quite the same with any business. We do not have to bother about overproduction for some years to come, provided the prices are right. It is the refusal of people to buy on account of price that really stimulates real business. Then if we want to do business we have to get the prices down without hurting the quality. Thus price reduction forces us to learn improved and less wasteful methods of production. One big part of the discovery of what is "normal" in industry depends on managerial genius discovering better ways of doing things. If a man reduces his selling price to a point where he is making no profit or incurring a loss, then he simply is forced to discover how to make as good an article by a better method—making his new method produce the profit, and not producing a profit out of reduced wages or increased prices to the public.

It is not good management to take profits out of the workers or the buyers; make management produce the profits. Don't cheapen the product; don't cheapen the wage; don't overcharge the public. Put brains into the method, and more brains, and still more brains—do things better than ever before; and by this means all parties to business are served and benefited.

And all of this can always be done.

Money – Master or Servant?

In December, 1920, business the country over was marking time. More automobile plants were closed than were open and quite a number of those which were closed were completely in the charge of bankers. Rumours of bad financial condition were afloat concerning nearly every industrial company, and I became interested when the reports persisted that the Ford Motor Company not only needed money but could not get it. I have become accustomed to all kinds of rumours about our company—so much so, that nowadays I rarely deny any sort of rumour. But these reports differed from all previous ones. They were so exact and circumstantial. I learned that I had overcome my prejudice against borrowing and that I might be found almost any day down in Wall Street, hat in hand, asking for money. And rumour went even further and said that no one would give me money and that I might have to break up and go out of business.

It is true that we did have a problem. In 1919 we had borrowed $70,000,000 on notes to buy the full stock interest in the Ford Motor Company. On this we had $33,000,000 left to pay. We had $18,000,000 in income taxes due or shortly to become due to the Government, and also we intended to pay our usual bonus for the year to the workmen, which amounted to $7,000,000. Altogether, between January 1st and April 18, 1921, we had payments ahead totaling $58,000,000. We had only $20,000,000 in bank. Our balance sheet was more or less common knowledge and I suppose it was taken for granted that we could not raise the $38,000,000 needed without borrowing. For that is quite a large sum of money. Without the aid of Wall Street such a sum could not easily and quickly be raised. We were perfectly good for the money. Two years before we had borrowed $70,000,000. And since our whole property was unencumbered and we had no commercial debts, the matter of lending a large sum to us would not ordinarily have been a matter of moment. In fact, it would have been good banking business.

However, I began to see that our need for money was being industriously circulated as an evidence of impending failure. Then I began to suspect that, although the rumours came in news dispatches from all over the country, they might perhaps be traced to a single source. This belief was further strengthened when we were informed that a very fat financial editor was at Battle Creek sending out bulletins concerning the acuteness of our financial condition. Therefore, I took care not to deny a single rumour. We had made our financial plans and they did not include borrowing money.

I cannot too greatly emphasize that the very worst time to borrow money is when the banking people think that you need money. In the last chapter I outlined our financial principles. We simply applied those principles. We planned a thorough house-cleaning.

Go back a bit and see what the conditions were. Along in the early part of 1920 came the first indications that the feverish speculative business engendered by the war was not going to continue. A few concerns that had sprung out of the war and had no real reason for existence failed. People slowed down in their buying. Our own sales kept right along, but we knew that sooner or later they would drop off. I thought seriously of cutting prices, but the costs of manufacturing everywhere were out of control. Labour gave less and less in return for high wages. The suppliers of raw material refused even to think of coming back to earth. The very plain warnings of the storm went quite unheeded.

In June our own sales began to be affected. They grew less and less each month from June on until September. We had to do something to bring our product within the purchasing power of the public, and not only that, we had to do something drastic enough to demonstrate to the public that we were actually playing the game and not just shamming. Therefore in September we cut the price of the touring car from $575 to $440. We cut the price far below the cost of production, for we were still making from stock bought at boom prices. The cut created a considerable sensation. We received a deal of criticism. It was said that we were disturbing conditions.

That is exactly what we were trying to do. We wanted to do our part in bringing prices from an artificial to a natural level. I am firmly of the opinion that if at this time or earlier manufacturers and distributors had all made drastic cuts in their prices and had put through thorough house-cleanings we should not have so long a business depression. Hanging on in the hope of getting higher prices simply delayed adjustment. Nobody got the higher prices they hoped for, and if the losses had been taken all at once, not only would the productive and the buying powers of the country have become harmonized, but we should have been saved this long period of general idleness. Hanging on in the hope of higher prices merely made the losses greater, because those who hung on had to pay interest on their high-priced stocks and also lost the profits they might have made by working on a sensible basis. Unemployment cut down wage distribution and thus the buyer and the seller became more and more separated. There was a lot of flurried talk of arranging to give vast credits to Europe—the idea being that thereby the high-priced stocks might be palmed off. Of course the proposals were not put in any such crude fashion, and I think that quite a lot of people sincerely believed that if large credits were extended abroad even without a hope of the payment of either principal or interest, American business would somehow be benefited. It is true that if these credits were taken by American banks, those who had high-priced stocks might have gotten rid of them at a profit, but the banks would have acquired so much frozen credit that they would have more nearly resembled ice houses than banks. I suppose it is natural to hang on to the possibility of profits until the very last moment, but it is not good business.

Our own sales, after the cut, increased, but soon they began to fall off again. We were not sufficiently within the purchasing power of the country to make buying easy. Retail prices generally had not touched bottom. The public distrusted all prices. We laid our plans for another cut and we kept our production around one hundred thousand cars a month. This production was not justified by our sales but we wanted to have as much as possible of our raw material transformed into finished product before we shut down. We knew that we would have to shut down in order to take an inventory and clean house. We wanted to open with another big cut and to have cars on hand to supply the demand. Then the new cars could be built out of material bought at lower prices. We determined that we were going to get lower prices.

We shut down in December with the intention of opening again in about two weeks. We found so much to do that actually we did not open for nearly six weeks. The moment that we shut down the rumours concerning our financial condition became more and more active. I know that a great many people hoped that we should have to go out after money—for, were we seeking money, then we should have to come to terms. We did not ask for money. We did not want money. We had one offer of money. An officer of a New York bank called on me with a financial plan which included a large loan and in which also was an arrangement by which a representative of the bankers would act as treasurer and take charge of the finance of the company. Those people meant well enough, I am quite sure. We did not want to borrow money but it so happened that at the moment we were without a treasurer. To that extent the bankers had envisaged our condition correctly. I asked my son Edsel to be treasurer as well as president of the company. That fixed us up as to a treasurer, so there was really nothing at all that the bankers could do for us.

Then we began our house-cleaning. During the war we had gone into many kinds of war work and had thus been forced to depart from our principle of a single product. This had caused many new departments to be added. The office force had expanded and much of the wastefulness of scattered production had crept in. War work is rush work and is wasteful work. We began throwing out everything that did not contribute to the production of cars.

The only immediate payment scheduled was the purely voluntary one of a seven-million-dollar bonus to our workmen. There was no obligation to pay, but we wanted to pay on the first of January. That we paid out of our cash on hand.

Throughout the country we have thirty-five branches. These are all assembling plants, but in twenty-two of them parts are also manufactured. They had stopped the making of parts but they went on assembling cars. At the time of shutting down we had practically no cars in Detroit. We had shipped out all the parts, and during January the Detroit dealers actually had to go as far a field as Chicago and Columbus to get cars for local needs. The branches shipped to each dealer, under his yearly quota, enough cars to cover about a month's sales. The dealers worked hard on sales. During the latter part of January we called in a skeleton organization of about ten thousand men, mostly foremen, sub-foremen, and straw bosses, and we started Highland Park into production. We collected our foreign accounts and sold our by-products.

Then we were ready for full production. And gradually into full production we went—on a profitable basis. The house-cleaning swept out the waste that had both made the prices high and absorbed the profit. We sold off the useless stuff. Before we had employed fifteen men per car per day. Afterward we employed nine per car per day. This did not mean that six out of fifteen men lost their jobs. They only ceased being unproductive. We made that cut by applying the rule that everything and everybody must produce or get out.

We cut our office forces in halves and offered the office workers better jobs in the shops. Most of them took the jobs. We abolished every order blank and every form of statistics that did not directly aid in the production of a car. We had been collecting tons of statistics because they were interesting. But statistics will not construct automobiles—so out they went.

We took out 60 per cent. of our telephone extensions. Only a comparatively few men in any organization need telephones. We formerly had a foreman for every five men; now we have a foreman for every twenty men. The other foremen are working on machines.

We cut the overhead charge from $146 a car to $93 a car, and when you realize what this means on more than four thousand cars a day you will have an idea how, not by economy, not by wage-cutting, but by the elimination of waste, it is possible to make an "impossible" price. Most important of all, we found out how to use less money in our business by speeding up the turnover. And in increasing the turnover rate, one of the most important factors was the Detroit, Toledo, & Ironton Railroad— which we purchased. The railroad took a large place in the scheme of economy. To the road itself I have given another chapter.

We discovered, after a little experimenting, that freight service could be improved sufficiently to reduce the cycle of manufacture from twenty-two to fourteen days. That is, raw material could be bought, manufactured, and the finished product put into the hands of the distributor in (roughly) 33 per cent. less time than before. We had been carrying an inventory of around $60,000,000 to insure uninterrupted production. Cutting down the time one third released $20,000,000, or $1,200,000 a year in interest. Counting the finished inventory, we saved approximately $8,000,000 more—that is, we were able to release $28,000,000 in capital and save the interest on that sum.

On January 1st we had $20,000,000. On April 1st we had $87,300,000, or $27,300,000 more than we needed to wipe out all our indebtedness. That is what boring into the business did for us! This amount came to us in these items:

Cash on hand, January $20,000,000
Stock on hand turned into cash, January 1 to April 1 24,700,000
Speeding up transit of goods released 28,000,000
Collected from agents in foreign countries 3,000,000
Sale of by-products 3,700,000
Sale of Liberty Bonds 7,900,000

TOTAL $87,300,000

Now I have told about all this not in the way of an exploit, but to point out how a business may find resources within itself instead of borrowing, and also to start a little thinking as to whether the form of our money may not put a premium on borrowing and thus give far too great a place in life to the bankers.

We could have borrowed $40,000,000—more had we wanted to. Suppose we had borrowed, what would have happened? Should we have been better fitted to go on with our business? Or worse fitted? If we had borrowed we should not have been under the necessity of finding methods to cheapen production. Had we been able to obtain the money at 6 per cent. flat—and we should in commissions and the like have had to pay more than that— the interest charge alone on a yearly production of 500,000 cars would have amounted to about four dollars a car. Therefore we should now be without the benefit of better production and loaded with a heavy debt. Our cars would probably cost about one hundred dollars more than they do; hence we should have a smaller production, for we could not have so many buyers; we should employ fewer men, and in short, should not be able to serve to the utmost. You will note that the financiers proposed to cure by lending money and not by bettering methods. They did not suggest putting in an engineer; they wanted to put in a treasurer.

And that is the danger of having bankers in business. They think solely in terms of money. They think of a factory as making money, not goods. They want to watch the money, not the efficiency of production. They cannot comprehend that a business never stands still, it must go forward or go back. They regard a reduction in prices as a throwing away of profit instead of as a building of business.

Bankers play far too great a part in the conduct of industry. Most business men will privately admit that fact. They will seldom publicly admit it because they are afraid of their bankers. It required less skill to make a fortune dealing in money than dealing in production. The average successful banker is by no means so intelligent and resourceful a man as is the average successful business man. Yet the banker through his control of credit practically controls the average business man.

There has been a great reaching out by bankers in the last fifteen or twenty years—and especially since the war—and the Federal Reserve System for a time put into their hands an almost limitless supply of credit. The banker is, as I have noted, by training and because of his position, totally unsuited to the conduct of industry. If, therefore, the controllers of credit have lately acquired this very large power, is it not to be taken as a sign that there is something wrong with the financial system that gives to finance instead of to service the predominant power in industry? It was not the industrial acumen of the bankers that brought them into the management of industry. Everyone will admit that. They were pushed there, willy-nilly, by the system itself. Therefore, I personally want to discover whether we are operating under the best financial system.

Now, let me say at once that my objection to bankers has nothing to do with personalities. I am not against bankers as such. We stand very much in need of thoughtful men, skilled in finance. The world cannot go on without banking facilities. We have to have money. We have to have credit. Otherwise the fruits of production could not be exchanged. We have to have capital. Without it there could be no production. But whether we have based our banking and our credit on the right foundation is quite another matter.

It is no part of my thought to attack our financial system. I am not in the position of one who has been beaten by the system and wants revenge. It does not make the least difference to me personally what bankers do because we have been able to manage our affairs without outside financial aid. My inquiry is prompted by no personal motive whatsoever. I only want to know whether the greatest good is being rendered to the greatest number.

No financial system is good which favors one class of producers over another. We want to discover whether it is not possible to take away power which is not based on wealth creation. Any sort of class legislation is pernicious. I think that the country's production has become so changed in its methods that gold is not the best medium with which it may be measured, and that the gold standard as a control of credit gives, as it is now (and I believe inevitably) administered, class advantage. The ultimate check on credit is the amount of gold in the country, regardless of the amount of wealth in the country.

I am not prepared to dogmatize on the subject of money or credit. As far as money and credit are concerned, no one as yet knows enough about them to dogmatize. The whole question will have to be settled as all other questions of real importance have to be settled, and that is by cautious, well-founded experiment. And I am not inclined to go beyond cautious experiments. We have to proceed step by step and very carefully. The question is not political, it is economic, and I am perfectly certain that helping the people to think on the question is wholly advantageous. They will not act without adequate knowledge, and thus cause disaster, if a sincere effort is made to provide them with knowledge. The money question has first place in multitudes of minds of all degrees or power. But a glance at most of the cure-all systems shows how contradictory they are. The majority of them make the assumption of honesty among mankind, to begin with, and that, of course, is a prime defect. Even our present system would work splendidly if all men were honest. As a matter of fact, the whole money question is 95 per cent. human nature; and your successful system must check human nature, not depend upon it.

The people are thinking about the money question; and if the money masters have any information which they think the people ought to have to prevent them going astray, now is the time to give it. The days are fast slipping away when the fear of credit curtailment will avail, or when wordy slogans will affright. The people are naturally conservative. They are more conservative than the financiers. Those who believe that the people are so easily led that they would permit printing presses to run off money like milk tickets do not understand them. It is the innate conservation of the people that has kept our money good in spite of the fantastic tricks which the financiers play—and which they cover up with high technical terms.

The people are on the side of sound money. They are so unalterably on the side of sound money that it is a serious question how they would regard the system under which they live, if they once knew what the initiated can do with it.

The present money system is not going to be changed by speech-making or political sensationalism or economic experiment. It is going to change under the pressure of conditions—conditions that we cannot control and pressure that we cannot control. These conditions are now with us; that pressure is now upon us.

The people must be helped to think naturally about money. They must be told what it is, and what makes it money, and what are the possible tricks of the present system which put nations and peoples under control of the few.

Money, after all, is extremely simple. It is a part of our transportation system. It is a simple and direct method of conveying goods from one person to another. Money is in itself most admirable. It is essential. It is not intrinsically evil. It is one of the most useful devices in social life. And when it does what it was intended to do, it is all help and no hindrance.

But money should always be money. A foot is always twelve inches, but when is a dollar a dollar? If ton weights changed in the coal yard, and peck measures changed in the grocery, and yard sticks were to-day 42 inches and to-morrow 33 inches (by some occult process called "exchange") the people would mighty soon remedy that. When a dollar is not always a dollar, when the 100-cent dollar becomes the 65-cent dollar, and then the 50-cent dollar, and then the 47-cent dollar, as the good old American gold and silver dollars did, what is the use of yelling about "cheap money," "depreciated money"? A dollar that stays 100 cents is as necessary as a pound that stays 16 ounces and a yard that stays 36 inches.

The bankers who do straight banking should regard themselves as naturally the first men to probe and understand our monetary system—instead of being content with the mastery of local banking-house methods; and if they would deprive the gamblers in bank balances of the name of "banker" and oust them once for all from the place of influence which that name gives them, banking would be restored and established as the public service it ought to be, and the iniquities of the present monetary system and financial devices would be lifted from the shoulders of the people.

There is an "if" here, of course. But it is not insurmountable. Affairs are coming to a jam as it is, and if those who possess technical facility do not engage to remedy the case, those who lack that facility may attempt it. Nothing is more foolish than for any class to assume that progress is an attack upon it. Progress is only a call made upon it to lend its experience for the general advancement. It is only those who are unwise who will attempt to obstruct progress and thereby become its victims. All of us are here together, all of us must go forward together; it is perfectly silly for any man or class to take umbrage at the stirring of progress. If financiers feel that progress is only the restlessness of weak-minded persons, if they regard all suggestions of betterment as a personal slap, then they are taking the part which proves more than anything else could their unfitness to continue in their leadership.

If the present faulty system is more profitable to a financier than a more perfect system would be, and if that financier values his few remaining years of personal profits more highly than he would value the honour of making a contribution to the life of the world by helping to erect a better system, then there is no way of preventing a clash of interests. But it is fair to say to the selfish financial interests that, if their fight is waged to perpetuate a system just because it profits them, then their fight is already lost. Why should finance fear? The world will still be here. Men will do business with one another. There will be money and there will be need of masters of the mechanism of money. Nothing is going to depart but the knots and tangles. There will be some readjustments, of course. Banks will no longer be the masters of industry. They will be the servants of industry. Business will control money instead of money controlling business. The ruinous interest system will be greatly modified. Banking will not be a risk, but a service. Banks will begin to do much more for the people than they do now, and instead of being the most expensive businesses in the world to manage, and the most highly profitable in the matter of dividends, they will become less costly, and the profits of their operation will go to the community which they serve.

Two facts of the old order are fundamental. First: that within the nation itself the tendency of financial control is toward its largest centralized banking institutions—either a government bank or a closely allied group of private financiers. There is always in every nation a definite control of credit by private or semi-public interests. Second: in the world as a whole the same centralizing tendency is operative. An American credit is under control of New York interests, as before the war world credit was controlled in London—the British pound sterling was the standard of exchange for the world's trade.

Two methods of reform are open to us, one beginning at the bottom and one beginning at the top. The latter is the more orderly way, the former is being tried in Russia. If our reform should begin at the top it will require a social vision and an altruistic fervour of a sincerity and intensity which is wholly inconsistent with selfish shrewdness.

The wealth of the world neither consists in nor is adequately represented by the money of the world. Gold itself is not a valuable commodity. It is no more wealth than hat checks are hats. But it can be so manipulated, as the sign of wealth, as to give its owners or controllers the whip-hand over the credit which producers of real wealth require. Dealing in money, the commodity of exchange, is a very lucrative business. When money itself becomes an article of commerce to be bought and sold before real wealth can be moved or exchanged, the usurers and speculators are thereby permitted to lay a tax on production. The hold which controllers of money are able to maintain on productive forces is seen to be more powerful when it is remembered that, although money is supposed to represent the real wealth of the world, there is always much more wealth than there is money, and real wealth is often compelled to wait upon money, thus leading to that most paradoxical situation—a world filled with wealth but suffering want.

These facts are not merely fiscal, to be cast into figures and left there. They are instinct with human destiny and they bleed. The poverty of the world is seldom caused by lack of goods but by a "money stringency." Commercial competition between nations, which leads to international rivalry and ill-will, which in their turn breed wars— these are some of the human significations of these facts. Thus poverty and war, two great preventable evils, grow on a single stem.

Let us see if a beginning toward a better method cannot be made.

THE DEVELOPMENT OF PUBLIC UTILITIES
BY BURTON J. HENDRICK

The streets of practically all American cities, as they appeared in 1870 and as they appear today, present one of the greatest contrasts in our industrial development. Fifty years ago only a few flickering gas lamps lighted the most traveled thoroughfares. Only the most prosperous business houses and homes had even this expensive illumination; most obtained their artificial light from the new illuminant known as kerosene. But it was the mechanism of city transportation that would have looked the strangest in our eyes. New York City had built the world's first horse-car line in 1832, and since that year this peculiarly American contrivance has had the most extended development. In 1870, indeed, practically every city of any importance had one or more railways of this type. New York possessed thirty different companies, each operating an independent system. In Philadelphia, Chicago, St. Louis, and San Francisco the growth of urban transportation had been equally haphazard. The idea of combining the several street railways into one comprehensive corporation had apparently occurred to no one. The passengers, in their peregrinations through the city, had frequently to pay three or four fares; competition was thus the universal rule. The mechanical equipment similarly represented a primitive state of organization. Horses and mules, in many cases hideous physical specimens of their breeds, furnished the motive power. The cars were little "bobtailed" receptacles, usually badly painted and more often than not in a desperate state of disrepair. In many cities the driver presided as a solitary autocrat; the passengers on entrance deposited their coins in a little fare box. At night tiny oil lamps made the darkness visible; in winter time shivering passengers warmed themselves by pulling their coat collars and furs closely about their necks and thrusting their lower members into a heap of straw, piled almost a foot deep on the floor.

Who would have thought, forty years ago, that the lighting of these dark and dirty streets and the modernization of these local railway systems would have given rise to one of the most astounding chapters in our financial history and created hundreds, perhaps thousands, of millionaires? When Thomas A. Edison invented the incandescent light, and when Frank J. Sprague in 1887 constructed the first practicable urban trolley line, in Richmond, Virginia, they liberated forces that powerfully affected not only our social and economic life but our political institutions. These two inventions introduced anew phrase—"Public Utilities." Combined with the great growth and prosperity of the cities they furnished a fruitful opportunity to several particularly famous groups of financial adventurers. They led to the organization of "syndicates" which devoted all their energies, for a quarter of a century, to exploiting city lighting and transportation systems. These syndicates made a business of entering city after city, purchasing the scattered street railway lines and lighting companies, equipping them with electricity, combining them into unified systems, organizing large corporations, and floating huge issues of securities. A single group of six men—Yerkes, Widener, Elkins, Dolan, Whitney, and Ryan—combined the street railways, and in many cases the lighting companies, of New York, Philadelphia, Chicago, Pittsburgh, and at least a hundred towns and cities in Pennsylvania, Connecticut, Rhode Island, Massachusetts, Ohio, Indiana, New Hampshire, and Maine. Either jointly or separately they controlled the gas and electric lighting companies of Philadelphia, Reading, Harrisburg, Atlanta, Vicksburg, St. Augustine, Minneapolis, Omaha, Des Moines, Kansas City, Sioux City, Syracuse, and about seventy other communities. A single corporation developed nearly all the trolley lines and lighting companies of New Jersey; another controlled similar utilities in San Francisco and other cities on the Pacific Coast. In practically all instances these syndicates adopted precisely the same plan of operation. In so far as their activities resulted in cheap, comfortable, rapid, and comprehensive transit systems and low-priced illumination, their activities greatly benefited the public. The future historian of American society will probably attribute enormous influence to the trolley car in linking urban community with urban community, in extending the radius of the modern city, in freeing urban workers from the demoralizing influences of the tenement, in offering the poorer classes comfortable homes in the surrounding country, and in extending general enlightenment by bringing about a closer human intercourse. Indeed, there is probably no single influence that has contributed so much to the pleasure and comfort of the masses as the trolley car.

Yet the story that I shall have to tell is not a pleasant one. It is impossible to write even a brief outline of this development without plunging deeply into the two phases of American life of which we have most cause to be ashamed; these are American municipal politics and the speculative aspects of Wall Street. The predominating influences in American city life have been the great franchise corporations. Practically all the men that have had most to do with developing our public utilities have also had the greatest influence in city politics. In New York, Thomas F. Ryan and William C. Whitney were the powerful, though invisible, powers in Tammany Hall. In Chicago, Charles T. Yerkes controlled mayors and city councils; he even extended his influence into the state government, controlling governors and legislatures. In Philadelphia, Widener and Elkins dominated the City Hall and also became part of the Quay machine of Pennsylvania. Mark Hanna, the most active force in Cleveland railways, was also the political boss of the State. Roswell P. Flower, chief agent in developing Brooklyn Rapid Transit, had been Governor of New York; Patrick Calhoun, who monopolized the utilities of San Francisco and other cities, presided likewise over the city's inner politics. The Public Service Corporation of New Jersey also comprised a large political power in city and state politics. It is hardly an exaggeration to say that in the most active period, that from 1880 to 1905, the powers that developed city railway and lighting companies in American cities were identically the same owners that had the most to do with city government. In the minds of these men politics was necessarily as much a part of their business as trolley poles and steel rails. This type of capitalist existed only on public franchises—the right to occupy the public streets with their trolley cars, gas mains, and electric light conduits; they could obtain these privileges only from complaisant city governments, and the simplest way to obtain them was to control these governments themselves. Herein we have the simple formula which made possible one of the most profitable and one of the most adventurous undertakings of our time.

An attempt to relate the history of all these syndicates would involve endless repetition. If we have the history of one we have the history of practically all. I have therefore selected, as typical, the operations of the group that developed the street railways and, to a certain extent, the public lighting companies, in our three greatest American cities—New York, Chicago, and Philadelphia.

One of the men who started these enterprises actually had a criminal record. William H. Kemble, an early member of the Philadelphia group, had been indicted for attempting to bribe the Pennsylvania Legislature; he had been convicted and sentenced to one year in the county jail and had escaped imprisonment only by virtue of a pardon obtained through political influence. Charles T. Yerkes, one of his partners in politics and street railway enterprises, had been less fortunate, for he had served seven months for assisting in the embezzlement of Philadelphia funds in 1873. It was this circumstance in Yerkes's career which impelled him to leave Philadelphia and settle in Chicago where, starting as a small broker, he ultimately acquired sufficient resources and influence to embark in that street railway business at which he had already served an extensive apprenticeship. Under his domination, the Chicago aldermen attained a gravity that made them notorious all over the world. They openly sold Yerkes the use of the streets for cash and constantly blocked the efforts which an infuriated populace made for reform. Yerkes purchased the old street railway lines, lined his pockets by making contracts for their reconstruction, issued large flotations of watered stock, heaped securities upon securities and reorganization upon reorganization and diverted their assets to business in a hundred ingenious ways.

In spite of the crimes which Yerkes perpetrated in American cities, there was something refreshing and ingratiating about the man. Possibly this is because he did not associate any hypocrisy with his depredations. "The secret of success in my business," he once frankly said, "is to buy old junk, fix it up a little, and unload it upon other fellows." Certain of his epigrams—such as, "It is the strap-hanger who pays the dividends"—have likewise given him a genial immortality. The fact that, after having reduced the railway system of Chicago to financial pulp and physical dissolution, he finally unloaded the whole useless mass, at a handsome personal profit, upon his old New York friends, Whitney and Ryan, and decamped to London, where he carried through huge transit enterprises, clearly demonstrated that Yerkes was a buccaneer of no ordinary caliber.

Yerkes's difficulties in Philadelphia indirectly made possible the career of Peter A. B. Widener. For Yerkes had become involved in the defalcation of the City Treasurer, Joseph P. Mercer, whose translation to the Eastern Penitentiary left vacant a municipal office into which Mr. Widener now promptly stepped. Thus Mr. Widener, as is practically the case with all these street railway magnates, was a municipal politician before he became a financier. The fact that he attained the city treasurership shows that he had already gone far, for it was the most powerful office in Philadelphia. He had all those qualities of suavity, joviality, firmness, and personal domination that made possible success in American local politics a generation ago. His occupation contributed to his advancement. In recent years Mr. Widener, as the owner of great art galleries and the patron of philanthropic and industrial institutions, has been a national figure of the utmost dignity. Had you dropped into the Spring Garden Market in Philadelphia forty years ago, you would have found a portly gentleman, clad in a white apron, and armed with a cleaver, presiding over a shop decorated with the design—"Peter A. B. Widener, Butcher." He was constantly joking with his customers and visitors, and in the evening he was accustomed to foregather with a group of well-chosen spirits who had been long famous in Philadelphia as the "all-night poker players." A successful butcher shop in Philadelphia in those days played about the same part in local politics as did the saloon in New York City. Such a station became the headquarters of political gossip and the meeting ground of a political clique; and so Widener, the son of a poor German bricklayer, rapidly became a political leader in the Twentieth Ward, and soon found his power extending even to Harrisburg. A few years ago Widener presided over a turbulent meeting of Metropolitan shareholders in Newark, New Jersey. The proposal under consideration was the transference of all the Metropolitan's visible assets to a company of which the stockholders knew nothing. When several of these stockholders arose and demanded that they be given an opportunity to discuss the projected lease, Widener turned to them and said, in his politest and blandest manner: "You can vote first and discuss afterward." Widener displayed precisely these same qualities of ingratiating arrogance and good-natured contempt as a Philadelphia politician. He was a man of big frame, alert and decisive in his movements, and a ready talker; in business he was given much to living in the clouds—a born speculator—emphatically a "boomer." His sympathies were generous, at times emotional; it is said that he has even been known to weep when discussing his fine collection of Madonnas. He showed this personal side in his lifelong friendship and business association with William L. Elkins, a man much inferior to him in ability. Indeed, Elkins's great fortune was little more than a free gift from Widener, who carried him as a partner in all his deals. Elkins became Widener's bondsman when the latter entered the City Treasurer's office; the two men lived near each other on the same street, and this association was cemented when Widener's oldest son married Elkins's daughter. Elkins had started life as an entry clerk in a grocery store, had made money in the butter and egg business, had "struck oil" at Titusville in 1862, and had succeeded in exchanging his holdings for a block of Standard Oil stock. He too became a Philadelphia politician, but he had certain hard qualities—he was close-fisted, slow, plodding—that prevented him from achieving much success.

For the other members of this group we must now change the scene to New York City. In the early eighties certain powerful interests had formed plans for controlling the New York transit fields. Prominent among them was William Collins Whitney, a very different type of man from the Philadelphians. Born in Conway, Massachusetts, in 1841, he came from a long line of distinguished and intellectual New Englanders. At Yale his wonderful mental gifts raised him far above his fellows; he divided all scholastic honors there with his classmate, William Graham Sumner, afterwards Yale's great political economist. Soon after graduation Whitney came to New York and rapidly forged ahead as a lawyer. Brilliant, polished, suave, he early displayed those qualities which afterward made him the master mind of presidential Cabinets and the maker of American Presidents. Physically handsome, loved by most men and all women, he soon acquired a social standing that amounted almost to a dictatorship. His early political activities had greatly benefited New York. He became a member of that group which, under the leadership of Joseph H. Choate and Samuel J. Tilden, accomplished the downfall of William M. Tweed. Whitney remained Tilden's political protege for several years. Though highbred and luxury-loving, as a young man he was not averse to hard political work, and many old-timers still remember the days when "Bill" Whitney delivered cart-tail harangues on the lower east side. By 1884 he had become the most prominent Democrat in New York—always a foe to Tammany—and as such he contributed largely to Cleveland's first election, became Secretary of the Navy in Cleveland's cabinet and that great President's close friend and adviser. As Secretary of the Navy, Whitney, who found the fleet composed of a few useless hulks left over from the days of Farragut, created the fighting force that did such efficient service in the Spanish War. The fact that the United States is now the third naval power is largely owing to these early activities of Whitney.

Certainly all this national service forms a strange prelude to Whitney's activities in the public utilities of New York and other cities. Had he died, indeed, in his fiftieth year, his name would be renowned today as a worker for the highest ideals of American citizenship. What suddenly made him turn his back upon his past, join his former enemies in Tammany Hall, and engage in these great speculative enterprises? The simplest explanation is that, with his ability and ambition, Whitney had the luxurious tastes of a Medici. At the height of his career his financial success found expression in a magnificent house which he established on Fifth Avenue. Its furnishings were one of the wonders of New York. Whitney ransacked the art treasures of Europe, stripped medieval castles of their carvings and tapestries, ripped whole staircases and ceilings from the repose of centuries, and relaid them in this abode of splendor, and here he entertained with a lavishness that astounded New York. This single exploit pictures the man. Everything that Whitney did and was his house, his financial transactions, his Wall Street speculations, the rewards which he gave his friends assumed heroic proportions. But these things all demanded money. The dilapidated horse railways of New York offered him his most convenient opportunity for amassing it.

But Whitney had not proceeded far when he came face to face with a quiet and energetic young man who had already made considerable progress in the New York transit field. This was a Virginian of South Irish descent who had started life as a humble broker's clerk twelve or fourteen years before. His name was Thomas Fortune Ryan. Few men have wielded

65

greater power in American finance, but in 1884 Ryan was merely a ruddy-faced, cleancut, and clean-living Irishman of thirty-three, who could be depended on to execute quickly and faithfully orders on the New York Stock Exchange—even though they were small ones—and who, in unostentatious fashion, had already acquired much influence in Tammany Hall. With his six feet of stature, his extremely slender figure, his long legs, his long arms, his raiment—which always represented the height of fashion and tended slightly toward the flashy—Ryan made a conspicuous figure wherever he went. He was born in 1851, on a small farm in Nelson County, Virginia. The Civil War, which broke out when Ryan was a boy of ten, destroyed the family fortune and in 1868, when seventeen, he began life as a dry-goods clerk in Baltimore, fulfilling the tradition of the successful country boy in the large city by marrying his employer's daughter. When his father-in-law failed, in 1870, Ryan came to New York, went to work in a broker's office, and succeeded so well that, in a few years, he was able to purchase a seat on the Stock Exchange. He was sufficiently skillful as a broker to number Jay Gould among his customers and to inspire a prophecy by William C. Whitney that, if he retained his health, he would become one of the richest men in the country. Afterwards, when he knew him more intimately, Whitney elaborated this estimate by saying that Ryan was "the most adroit, suave, and noiseless man he had ever known." Ryan had two compelling traits that soon won for him these influential admirers. First of all was his marvelous industry. His genius was not spasmodic. He worked steadily, regularly, never losing a moment, never getting excited, going, day after day, the same monotonous dog-trot, easily outdistancing scores of apparently stronger men. He also had the indispensable faculty of silence. He has always been the least talkative man in Wall Street, but, with all his reserve, he has remained the soul of courtesy and outward good nature.

Here, then, we have the characters of this great impending drama—Yerkes in Chicago, Widener and Elkins in Philadelphia, Whitney and Ryan in New York. These five men did not invariably work as a unit. Yerkes, though he had considerable interest in Philadelphia, which had been the scene of his earliest exploits, limited his activities largely to Chicago. Widener and Elkins, however, not only dominated Philadelphia traction but participated in all of Yerkes's enterprises in Chicago and held an equal interest with Whitney and Ryan in New York. The latter Metropolitan pair, though they confined their interest chiefly to their own city, at times transferred their attention to Chicago. Thus, for nearly thirty years, these five men found their oyster in the transit systems of America's three greatest cities—and, for that matter, in many others also.

An attempt to trace the convolutions of America's street railway and public lighting finance would involve a puzzling array of statistics and an inextricable complexity of stocks, bonds, leases, holding companies, operating companies, construction companies, reorganizations, and the like. Difficult and apparently impenetrable as is this financial morass, the essential facts still stand out plainly enough. As already indicated, the fundamental basis upon which the whole system rested was the control of municipal politics. The story of the Metropolitan's manipulation of the New York street railways starts with one of the most sordid episodes in the municipal annals of America's largest city. Somewhat more than thirty years ago, a group of New York city fathers acquired an international fame as the "boodle aldermen." These men had finally given way to the importunities of a certain Jacob Sharp, an eccentric New York character, who had for many years operated New York City railways, and granted a franchise for the construction of a horse-car line on lower Broadway. Soon after voting this franchise, regarded as perhaps the most valuable in the world, these same aldermen had begun to wear diamonds, to purchase real estate, and give other outward evidences of unexpected prosperity. Presently, however, these city fathers started a migration to Canada, Mexico, Spain, and other countries where the processes of extradition did not work smoothly. Sharp's enemies had succeeded in precipitating a legislative investigation under the very capable leadership of Roscoe Conkling, who had little difficulty in showing that Sharp had purchased his aldermen for $500,000 cash. In a short time, such of the aldermen as were accessible to the police were languishing in prison, and Sharp had been arrested on twenty-one indictments for bribery and sentenced to four years' hard labor—a sentence which he was saved from serving by his lonely and miserable death in Ludlow Street Jail. In the delirium preceding his dissolution Sharp raved constantly about his Broadway railroad and his enemies; it was apparently his belief that the investigation which had uncovered his rascality and the subsequent "persecutions" had been engineered by certain of his rivals, either to compel Sharp to disgorge his franchise or to produce the facts that would justify the legislature in annulling it on the ground of fraud.

Though the complete history of this transaction can never be written, we do possess certain facts that lend some color to this diagnosis. Up to the time that Sharp had captured this franchise, Ryan, Whitney, and the Philadelphians—not as partners, but as rivals—had competed with him for this prize. At the trial of Arthur J. McQuade in 1886, a fellow conspirator, who bore the somewhat suggestive name of Fullgraff, related certain details which, if true, would indicate that Sharp's methods differed from those of his rivals only in that they had proved more successful. Thirteen members of the Board of Aldermen, said Fullgraff, had formed a close corporation, elected a chairman, and adopted a policy of "business unity in all important matters," which meant that they proposed to keep together in order to secure the highest price for the Broadway franchise. The cable railroad, which was the one with which Mr. Ryan was identified, offered $750,000, half in bonds and half in cash. Mr. Sharp, however, offered $500,000 all in cash. The aldermen voted in favor of Sharp because cash was not only a more valuable commodity than the bonds but, to use Alderman Fullgraff's own words—"less easily traced." That Whitney financed lawsuits against the validity of Sharp's franchise appears upon the record, and that Ryan was actively promoting the Conkling investigation, is likewise a matter of evidence. Sharp's victory had the great result of bringing together the three forces—Ryan, Whitney, and the Philadelphians—who had hitherto combated one another as rivals; that is, it caused the organization of the famous Whitney-Ryan-Widener-Elkins syndicate. If these men had inspired all those attacks on Sharp, their maneuver proved successful; for when the investigation had attained its climax and public indignation against Sharp had reached its most furious stage, that venerable corruptionist, worn down by ill health, and almost crazed by the popular outcry, sold his Broadway railroad to Peter A. B. Widener, William L. Elkins, and William H. Kemble. Thomas F. Ryan became secretary of the new corporation, and William C. Whitney an active participant in its affairs.

This Broadway franchise formed the vertebral column of the New York transit system; with it as a basis, the operators formed the Metropolitan Street Railway Company in 1893, commonly known as the "Metropolitan." They organized also the Metropolitan Traction Company, an organization which enjoys an historic position as the first "holding company" ever created in this country. Its peculiar attribute was that it did not construct and operate street railways itself, but merely owned other corporations that did so. Its only assets, that is, were paper securities representing the ownership and control of other companies. This "holding company," which has since become almost a standardized form of corporation control in this country, was the invention of Mr. Francis Lynde Stetson, one of America's greatest corporation lawyers. "Mr. Stetson," Ryan is said to have remarked, "do you know what you did when you drew up the papers of the Metropolitan Traction Company? You made us a great big tin box."

The plan which Whitney and his associates now followed was to obtain control, in various ways, of all the surface railways in New York and place them under the leadership of the Metropolitan. Through their political influences they obtained franchises of priceless value, organized subsidiary street railway companies, and exchanged the stock of these subsidiary companies for that of the Metropolitan. A few illustrations will show the character of these transactions. They thus acquired, practically as a free gift, a franchise to build a cable railroad on Lexington Avenue. At an extremely liberal estimate, this line cost perhaps $2,500,000 to construct, yet the syndicate turned this over to the Metropolitan for $10,000,000 of Metropolitan securities. They similarly acquired a franchise for a line on

Columbus Avenue, spending perhaps $500,000 in construction, and handing the completed property over to the Metropolitan for $6,000,000. In exchange for these two properties, representing a real investment, it has been maintained, of $3,000,000, the inside syndicates received securities which had a face value of $16,000,000 and which, as will appear subsequently, had a market cash value of not far from $25,000,000. They purchased an old horse-car line on Fulton Street, a line whose assets consisted of one-third of a mile of tracks, ten little box cars, thirty horses, and an operating deficit of $40,000 a year. At auction, its visible assets might have brought $15,000; yet the syndicate turned this over to the Metropolitan for $1,000,000. They spent $50,000 in constructing and equipping a horse railroad on Twenty-eighth and Twenty-ninth Streets and turned this over to the Metropolitan for $3,000,000. For two and a half miles of railroad on Thirty-fourth Street, which represented a cash expenditure of perhaps $100,000, they received $2,000,000 of Metropolitan stock. But it is hardly necessary to catalogue more instances; the plan of operations must now be fairly evident. It was for the members of the syndicate, as individuals, to collect all the properties and new franchises that were available and to transfer them to the Metropolitan at enormously inflated values. So far, all these deals were purely stock transactions—no cash had yet changed hands. When the amalgamation was complete, the insiders found themselves in possession of large amounts of Metropolitan stock.

Nearly all the properties actually purchased and transferred in the manner described above, had little earning capacity, and therefore little value; they were decrepit horse-car lines in unprofitable territory. The really valuable roads were those that traversed the great north and south thoroughfares—Lenox, Third, Fourth, Sixth, Eighth, and Ninth Avenues. Many old New York families and estates had held these properties for years and had collected large annual dividends from them. Naturally they had no desire to sell, yet their acquisition was essential to the monopoly which the Whitney-Ryan syndicate aspired to construct. They finally leased all these roads, under agreements which guaranteed large annual rentals. In practically all these cases the Metropolitan, in order to secure physical possession, agreed to pay rentals that far exceeded the earning capacity of the road. What is the explanation of such insane finance? We do not have the precise facts in the matter of the New York railways; but similar operations in Chicago, which have been officially made public, shed the utmost light upon the situation. In order to get possession of a single road in Chicago, Widener and Elkins guaranteed a thirty-five per cent dividend; to get one Philadelphia line, they guaranteed 65 1/2 per cent on capital paid in. This, of course, was not business; the motives actuating the syndicate were purely speculative. In Chicago, Widener and Elkins quietly made large purchases of the stock in these roads before they leased them to the parent company. The exceedingly profitable lease naturally gave such stocks a high value, in case they preferred to sell; if they held them, they reaped huge rewards from the leases which they had themselves decreed. Perhaps their most remarkable exploit was the lease of the West Division Railway Company of Chicago to the West Chicago Street Railroad. Widener and Elkins controlled the West Division Railway; their partner, Charles T. Yerkes, controlled the latter corporation. The negotiation of a lease, therefore, was a purely informal matter; the partners were merely dealing with one another; yet Widener and Elkins received a fee of $5,000,000 as personal compensation for negotiating this lease!

But this whole leasing system, both in New York and Chicago, entailed scandals perhaps even more reprehensible. All these leased properties, when taken over, were horse-car lines, and their transformation into electrically propelled systems involved reconstruction operations on an extensive scale. It seems perfectly clear that the chief motive which inspired these extravagant leases was the determination of the individuals who made up the syndicate to obtain physical possession and to make huge profits on construction. The "construction accounts" of the Metropolitan in New York form the most mysterious and incredible chapter in its history. The Metropolitan reports show that they spent anywhere from $500,000 to $600,000 a mile building underground trolley lines which, at their own extravagant estimate, should have cost only $150,000. In a few years untold millions, wasted in this way, disappeared from the Metropolitan treasury. In 1907 the Public Service Commission of New York began investigating these "construction accounts," but it had not proceeded far when the discovery was made that all the Metropolitan books containing the information desired had been destroyed. All the ledgers, journals, checks, and vouchers containing the financial history of the Metropolitan since its organization in 1893 had been sold for $117 to a junkman, who had agreed in writing to grind them into pulp, so that they would be safe from "prying eyes." We shall therefore never know precisely how this money was spent. But here again the Chicago transactions help us to an understanding. In 1898 Charles T. Yerkes, with that cynical frankness which some people have regarded as a redeeming trait in his character, opened his books for the preceding twenty-five years to the Civic Federation of Chicago. These books disclosed that Mr. Yerkes and his associates, Widener and Elkins, had made many millions in reconstructing the Chicago lines at prices which represented gross overcharges to the stockholders. For this purpose Yerkes, Widener, and Elkins organized the United States Construction Company and made contracts for installing the new electric systems on the lines which they controlled by lease or stock ownership. It seems a not unnatural suspicion that the vanished Metropolitan books would have disclosed similar performances in New York.

The concluding chapter of this tragedy has its setting in the Stock Exchange. These inside gentlemen, as already said, received no cash as their profits from these manipulations—only stock. But in the eyes of the public this stock represented an enormous value. Metropolitan securities, for example, represented the control and ownership of all the surface transit business in the city of New York. Naturally, it had a great investment value. When it began to pay regularly seven per cent dividends, the public appetite for Metropolitan became insatiable. The eager purchasers did not know, what we know now, that the Metropolitan did not earn these dividends and never could have earned them. The mere fact that it was paying, as rentals on its leased lines, annual sums far in excess of their earning capacity, necessarily prevented anything in the nature of profitable operation. The unpleasant fact is that these dividends were paid with borrowed money merely to make the stock marketable. It is not unlikely that the padded construction accounts, already described, may have concealed large disbursements of money for unearned dividends. When the Metropolitan was listed in 1897, it immediately went beyond par. The excitement that followed forms one of the most memorable chapters in the history of Wall Street. The investing public, egged on by daring and skillful stock manipulators, simply went mad and purchased not only Metropolitan but street railway shares that were then even more speculative. It was in these bubble days that Brooklyn Rapid Transit soared to heights from which it subsequently descended precipitately. Under this stimulus, Metropolitan stock ultimately sold at $269 a share. While the whole investing public was scrambling for Metropolitan, the members of the exploiting syndicate found ample opportunity to sell. The real situation became apparent when William C. Whitney died in 1904 leaving an estate valued at $40,000,000. Not a single share of Metropolitan was found among his assets! The final crash came in 1907, when the Metropolitan, a wrecked and plundered shell, confessed insolvency and went into a receivership. Those who had purchased its stock found their holdings as worthless as the traditional western gold mine. The story of the Chicago and Philadelphia systems, as well as that of numerous other cities, had been essentially the same. The transit facilities of millions of Americans had merely become the instruments of a group of speculators who had made huge personal fortunes and had left, as a monument of their labors, street railway lines whose gross overcapitalization was apparent to all and whose physical dilapidation in many cases revealed the character of their management.

It seems perhaps an exaggeration to say that the enterprises which have resulted in equipping our American cities and suburbs with trolley lines and electric lighting facilities have followed the plan of campaign sketched above. Perhaps not all have repeated the worst excesses of the syndicate that so remorselessly exploited New York, Chicago, and Philadelphia. Yet in most cases these elaborate undertakings have been largely speculative in character. Huge issues of fictitious stock, created purely for the benefit of inner rings, have been almost the prevailing rule. Stock speculation and municipal corruption have constantly gone hand in hand everywhere with the development of the public utilities. The relation of franchise corporations to municipalities is probably the thing which has chiefly opened the eyes of Americans to certain glaring defects in their democratic organization. The popular agitation which has resulted has led to great political reforms. The one satisfaction which we can derive from such a relation as that given above is that, after all, it is representative of a past era in our political and economic life. No new "Metropolitan syndicate" can ever repeat the operations of its predecessors. Practically every State now has utility commissions which regulate the granting of franchises, the issue of securities, the details of construction and equipment and service. An awakened public conscience has effectively ended the alliance between politics and franchise corporations and the type of syndicate described in the foregoing pages belongs as much to our American past as that rude frontier civilization with which, after all, it had many characteristics in common.

THE BUSINESS CAREER IN ITS PUBLIC
RELATIONS
BY ALBERT SHAW, PH.D

The purpose of this discourse is to set forth some of the social and public aspects of trade and commerce in our modern life. We have heard much in these recent times concerning the State in its relation to trade, industry, and the economic concerns of individuals and groups. Rapidly changing conditions, however, make it fitting that more should be said from the opposite standpoint;—that is to say, regarding the responsibilities of the business community as such toward the State in particular and toward the whole social organism in general.

Some of the thoughts to which I should like to give expression might perhaps too readily fall into abstract or philosophical terms. They might, on the other hand, only too readily clothe themselves in cant phrases and assume the hortatory tone. I shall try to avoid dialectic or theory on the one hand, and preaching on the other. I take it that what I am to say is addressed chiefly to young men, and that it ought to serve a practical object.

In the universities the spirit of idealism dominates. The academic point of view is not merely an intellectual one, but it is also ethical and altruistic. In the business world, on the other hand, we are told that no success is possible except that which is based upon the motive of money-getting by any means, however ruthless. We are told that the standards of business life are in conflict irreconcilable with true idealistic aims. It is this situation that I wish to analyze and discuss; for it concerns the student in a very direct way.

Our moralists point out the dangerous prevalence of those low standards of personal life and conduct summed up in the term "commercialism." We are warned by some of our foremost teachers and ethical leaders against commercialism in politics and commercialism in society. So bitterly reprobated indeed is the influence of commercialism that it might be inferred that commerce itself is at best a necessary evil and a thing to be apologized for. But if we are to accept this point of view without careful discrimination, we may well be alarmed; for we live in a world given over as never before to the whirl of industry and the rush and excitement of the market-place.

This, of all ages, is the age of the business man. The heroic times when warfare was the chief concern of nations, have long since passed by. So too the ages of faith,—when theology was the mainspring of action, when whole peoples went on long crusades, and when building cathedrals and burning heretics were typical of men's efforts and convictions—have fallen far into the historic background. Further, we would seem in the main to have left behind us that period of which the French Revolution is the most conspicuous landmark, when the gaining of political liberty for the individual seemed the one supreme good, and the object for which nations and communities were ready to sacrifice all else.

Through these and other periods characterized by their own especial aims and ideals, we have come to an age when commercialism is the all-absorbing thing; and we are told by pessimists that these dominant conditions are hopelessly incompatible with academic idealism or with the maintenance of high ethical standards, whether for the guidance of the individual himself or for the acceptance and control of the community. It is precisely this state of affairs, then, that I desire briefly to consider. And I shall keep in mind those bearings of it that might seem to have some relation to the views and aims of students who are soon to go out from the sheltered life of the university,—under the necessity, whether they shrink from it or not, of becoming part and parcel of this organism of business and trade that has invaded almost every sphere of modern activity.

I have only recently heard a great and eloquent teacher of morals, himself an exponent of the highest and finest culture to which we have attained, speak in terms of the utmost doubt and anxiety regarding the drift of the times. To his mind, the evils and dangers accompanying the stupendous developments of our day are such as to set what he called commercialism in direct antagonism to all that in his mind represented the higher good, which he termed idealism. The impression that he left upon his audience was that the forces of our present-day business life are inherently opposed to the achievement of the best results in statecraft and in the general life of the community. He could propose no remedy for the evils he deplored except education, and the saving of the old ideals through the remnant of the faithful who had not bowed the knee in the temple of Mammon. But he pointed out no way by which to protect the tender blossoms of academic idealism, when they meet their inevitable exposure in due time to the blighting and withering blasts of the commercialism that to him seemed so little reconcilable with the good, the true, and the beautiful.

To all this the practical man can only reply, that if, indeed, commercialism itself cannot be made to furnish a soil and an atmosphere in which idealism can grow, bud, blossom, and bear glorious fruit,—then idealism is hopelessly a lost cause. If it be not possible to promote things ideally good through these very forces of commercial and industrial life, then the outlook is a gloomy one for the social moralist and the political purist.

It is not a defensive position that I propose to take. I should not think it needful at this time even so much as briefly to reflect any of those timorous and painful arguments *pro* and *con* that one finds at times running through the columns of the press, particularly of the religious weeklies, on such a question as, for example, whether nowadays a man can at the same time be a true Christian and a successful business man; or whether the observance of the principles of common honesty is at all compatible with a winning effort to make a decent living.

I am well aware that the thoughtful and intellectual founder of this lectureship, under which I have been invited to speak, takes no such narrow view either of morality on the one hand or of the function of business life on the other. His definition of morality in business would demand something very different from the mere avoidance of certain obvious transgressions of the accepted rules of conduct, particularly of that commandment which says: "Thou shalt not steal." Nor, on the other hand, would his definition of the functions of business life be in any manner bounded by the notion that business is a pursuit having for its sole object the getting of the largest possible amount of money.

Those people who are content to apply negative moral standards to the carrying on of business life remind one of the little boy's familiar definition of salt: "Salt," said he, "is what makes potatoes taste bad when you don't put any on." According to that sort of definition, morality in business would be defined as that quality which makes the grocer good and respectable when he resists temptation and does not put sand in the sugar. The smug maxim that honesty is the best policy, while doubtless true enough as a verdict of human experience under normal conditions, is not fitted to arouse much enthusiasm as a statement of ultimate ethical aims and ideals.

If it were admitted that the sole or guiding motive in a business career must needs be the accumulation of money, I should certainly not think it worth while, in the name of trade morals, to urge young men who are to enter business life that they play the game according to safe and well-recognized rules. I would not take the trouble to advise them to study the penal code and to familiarize themselves with the legal definitions of grand and petit larceny, of embezzlement, or fraud, or arson, in order that they might escape certain hazards that beset a too narrow kind of devotion to business success. It is true, doubtless, that a business career affords peculiar opportunities, and is therefore subject to its own characteristic temptations, as respects the purely private and personal standards of conduct.

The magnitude of our economic movement, the very splendor of the opportunities that the swift development of a vast young country like ours affords, must inevitably in some cases upset at once the sober business judgment of men, and in some cases the standard of personal honor and good faith, in the temptation to get rich quickly; so that wrong is done thereby to a man's associates or to those whose interests are in his hands, while still greater wrong is done to his own character.

But, even against this dangerous greed for wealth and the unscrupulousness and ruthlessness which it engenders, it is no part of my present object to warn any young man. I take it that the negative standards of private conduct are usually not much affected by a man's choice of a pursuit in life. If any man's honor could be filched from him by a merely pecuniary reward, whether greater or less, I should not think it likely that he would be much safer in the long run if he chose the clerical profession, for example, than if he went into business.

Sooner or later his character would disclose itself. It is not, then, of the private and negative standards of conduct that I wish to speak,—except by way of such allusions as these. And even these allusions are only for the sake of making more distinct the positive and active phases of business ethics that I should like to present in such a way as to fasten them upon the attention.

Many young men, to whom these views are addressed, will doubtless choose, or have already chosen, what is commonly known as a professional career. The ministry, law, and medicine are the oldest and best recognized of the so-called liberal or learned professions. Now what are the distinctive marks of professional life? Are the men who practice these professions not also business men? And if so, how are they different from those business men who are considered laymen, or non-professional? Obviously the distinctions that are to be drawn, if any, are in the nature of marked tendencies. We shall not expect to find any hard and fast lines. Many lawyers, some doctors, and a few clergymen are clearly enough business men, in the sense that they attach more importance to the economic bearings of the part they play in the social organism than to the higher ethical or intellectual aspects of their work.

I have read and heard many definitions of what really constitutes a professional man. Whatever else, however, may characterize the nature of his calling, it seems to me plain that no man can be thought a true or worthy member of a profession who does not admit, both in theory and in the rules and practices of his life, that he has a public function to serve, and that he must frequently be at some discomfort or disadvantage because of the calls of professional duty. The laborer is worthy of his hire; and the professional man is entitled to obtain, if he can, a competence for himself and his family from the useful and productive service he is rendering to his fellow men. He may even, through genius or through the great confidence his character and skill inspire, gain considerable wealth in the practice of his profession. But if he is a true professional man he does not derive his incentive to effort solely or chiefly from the pecuniary gains that his profession brings him. Nor is the amount of his income regarded among the fellow members of his profession as the true test or measure of his success.

Thus the lawyer, in the theory of his profession, bears an important public relation to the dispensing of justice and to the protection of the innocent and the feeble. He is not a private person, but a part of the system for supporting the reign of law and of right in the community. Historically, in this country, the lawyer has also borne a great part in the making and administering of our institutions of government. If, as some of us think, the ethical code of that profession needs to be somewhat revised in view of present-day conditions, and needs also to be more sternly applied to some of the members of the profession, it is true, none the less, that there clearly belongs to this great calling a series of duties of a public nature, some of them imposed by the laws of the land, and others inherent in the very nature of the occupation itself.

It is true in an even more marked and undeniable fashion that the profession of medicine, by virtue of its public and social aspects, is distinguished in a marked way from a calling in life in which a man might feel that what he did was strictly his own business, subject to nobody's scrutiny, or inquiry, or interference. The physician's public obligation is in part prescribed by the laws of the State which regulate medical practice, and in very large part by the professional codes which have been evolved by the profession itself for its own guidance. It is not the amount of his fee that the overworked doctor is thinking about when he risks his own health in response to night calls, or when he devotes himself to some especially painful or difficult case. Nor is it a mere consideration of his possible earnings that would deter him from seeking comfort and safety by taking his family to Europe at a time when an epidemic had broken out in his own neighborhood.

I need not allude to the unselfish devotion to the good of the community that in so high a degree marks the lives of most of the members of the clerical profession, for this is evident to all observant persons.

On the other hand, it cannot be too clearly perceived that there is nothing in the disinterestedness, and in the obligation to render public service characterizing professional life that amounts to unnatural self-denial or painful renunciation,—unless in some extreme and individual cases. On the contrary, professional life at its best offers a great advantage in so far as it permits a man to think first of the work he is doing and the social service he is rendering, rather than of pecuniary reward. I have myself on more than one occasion pointed out to young men the greater prospect for happiness in life that comes with the choice of a calling in which the work itself primarily focuses the attention, and in which the pecuniary reward comes as an incident rather than as the conscious and direct result of a given effort.

The greatest pleasure in work is that which comes from the trained and regulated exercise of the faculty of imagination. In the conduct of every law case this faculty has abundant opportunity, as it also has in the efforts of the physician to aid nature in the restoration of health and vigor in the individual, or in the sanitary protection of the community. I hope I have made clear this point: that pecuniary success, even in large measure, in the work of a professional man, may be entirely compatible with disinterested devotion to a kind of work that makes for the public weal, while it is also worthy of pursuit for its own sake, and brings content and even happiness in the doing. And it is clear enough, in the case of a professional man, that he is false to his profession and to his plain obligations if he shows himself to be ruled by the anti-social spirit; that is to say, if he considers himself absolved from any duties towards the community about him; thinks that the practice of his profession is a private affair for his own profit and advantage, and holds that he has done his whole duty when he has escaped liability for malpractice or disbarment.

But the three oldest and best recognized professions no longer stand alone, in the estimation of our higher educational authorities and of the intelligent public. In a democracy like ours, with a constantly advancing conception of what is involved in education for citizenship and for participation in every individual function of the social and economic life, the work of the teacher comes to be recognized as professional in the highest sense. Teaching, indeed, seems destined in the near future to become the very foremost of all the professions. This recognition will come when the idea takes full possession of the public mind that the chief task of each generation is to train the next one, and to transmit such stores of knowledge and useful experience as it has received from its predecessors or has evolved for itself.

It is obvious enough that the work of the teacher gives room for the play of the loftiest ideals, and that its functions are essentially public and disinterested. But there are other callings, such as those of the architect and engineer, which have also come to be spoken of as professional in their nature. Their kinship to the older professions has been more readily recognized by the men of conservative university traditions, because much of the preparation for these callings can advantageously be of an academic sort. Architecture in its historical aspects is closely associated with the study of classical periods; while the profession of the engineer relates itself to the immemorial university devotion to mathematics. And in like manner the man who for practical purposes becomes a chemist or an electrician would be easily admitted by President Eliot, for example, to the favored fellowship of the professional classes for the reason, first, of the disciplinary and liberalizing nature of the studies that underlie his calling, and, in the second place, of the public and social aspects of the functions he fulfils in the pursuit of his vocation.

The architect, the civil or mechanical or electrical engineer, and the chemist, as well as the professional teacher, the trained librarian, or the journalist who carries on his work with due sense of its almost unequaled public duties and responsibilities,—all these are now admitted by dicta of our foremost authorities to a place equal with the law, medicine, and the ministry in the list of the professions; that is to say, in the group of callings which, under my definition, are distinguished especially by their public character. And in this group, of course, should be included politicians, legislators, and public administrators in so far as they serve the public interests reputably and in a professional spirit. Nor should we forget such special classes of public servants as the officers of the army and navy; while nobody will deny public character and professional rank to men of letters, artists, musicians and actors.

In all these callings it is demanded not merely that men shall be subject to the private rules of conduct,—that they must not cheat, or lie, or steal, or bear false witness, or be bad neighbors or undesirable citizens,—but in addition and in the most important sense that they shall be subject to positive ethical standards that relate to the welfare of the whole community, and that require of them the exercise of a true public spirit.

The man of public spirit is he who is able at a given moment, under certain conditions, to set the public welfare before his own. Furthermore, he is a man who is trained and habituated to that point of view, so that he is not aware of any pangs of martyrdom or even of any exercise of self-denial when he is concerning himself about the public good even to his own momentary inconvenience or disadvantage. Public spirit is that state or habit of mind which leads a man to care greatly for the general welfare. It is this ethical quality that to my mind should be the great aim and object of training.

On its best side, what we term the professional spirit is, then, very closely related to this commendable quality in men of a right intellectual and moral development that we call public spirit. The chief difference lies in this: that whereas all professional men may be public-spirited in a general sense, each professional man should, in addition, manifest a special and technical sort of public spirit that pertains to the nature of his calling. The lawyer should have a particularly keen regard for the equitable administration of justice. The doctor should truly care for the physical wholesomeness and well-being of the community. The clergyman should be alive to those things that concern the rectitude and purity of life. The journalist should be willing to make sacrifices for the sake of the enlightenment of public opinion; and so on. Without either the general or the technical manifestations of public spirit, in short, the so-called professional man is a reproach to his guild and a failure in his neighborhood.

Now, what has all this to do with the moral standards that belong to the business career as distinguished from the professional life? My answer must be very clear and very direct if I am to justify so long an analysis of the ethical characteristics of the professions themselves. I have merely used the time-honored method of trying to lead you by way of familiar, admitted points of view to certain points of view that, if not wholly new, are at least less familiar and less widely recognized. The whole thesis that I wish to develop is simply this: that however it may have been in business life in times past and gone, there has been such a tremendous change in the organization and methods of the business world and also in the relative importance of the functions of the business man in the community, that the distinctions which have hitherto set apart the professional classes have become obsolete for all practical purposes in many branches and departments of the business world.

At least, the work of the responsible leaders is no longer to be regarded as essentially a thing of private concern and free from public responsibility. If the business world is not characterized, first, by public spirit and a sense of public duty in general, and, second, by the special and technical sense of public obligation that pertains to particular kinds or departments of business activity, then it is falling short of its best opportunities and evading its providential tasks. It is for the modern business world to recognize the conditions that have in the fulness of time given it so great a power and so dominant a position; and it must not shirk the responsibilities that belong to it as fully and truly as they belong to any of the professions.

I hold, then, that the young man of education and opportunity who proposes to go into a business career enters it not merely with a low and unworthy standard if his sole motive and object be to acquire wealth, but he also enters it in disregard of the ideas that fill the minds of the best modern business leaders. He shows a pitiable lack of appreciation of the elements that are to constitute real business success in the period within which his own career must fall.

Let us consider, briefly, the evolution of our present-day economic or business life, and then take note of the necessary place that particular classes of business men must hold in the structure of our society. I, for my part, look upon this last century of economic progress,—under the sway of what is often called "capitalism" as a term of reproach,—as an immeasurable boon to mankind. It began with the practical utilization of several great inventions, notably that of steam power, which broke up the old household and village industries, gave us the modern factory system, and along with the development of railroads gave us the modern industrial city. This new and revolutionizing system of industry and business forced its way into a world of poverty, of disease, of depraved public life, of low morals in the main pervading the community,—a world for the most part of class distinctions in which the lot even of the privileged few was not a very noble or enviable one, while the state of the vast majority was little better than that of serfs.

Many writers have sought to throw a charm and a glamour over that old condition of economic life and society that followed the break-up of feudalism and that preceded the creation of our new political and industrial institutions. But with some mitigations it was for most people a period, as I have said, of squalor, disease, and degradation. The fundamental trouble could be summed up in the one word, *poverty*. The mission of the new industrial system, for the most part unconscious and unrecognized, was to transform the world by abolishing the reign of poverty. Doubtless it would be desirable if the improvement of conditions, material and spiritual, could make progress with exactly even pace on some perfectly symmetrical plan. But history shows us that the forward social movement has proceeded first in one aspect, then in another, on lines so tangential, often so zigzag, that it is difficult until one gets distance enough for perspective, to see that any true progress has been made at all.

Thus, the modern industrial system, which found the conditions of poverty, disease, and hardship prevalent, seemed for quite a long time, in its rude breaking up of old relations and its ruthless adherence to certain newly proclaimed principles, to have brought matters from bad to worse. The squalor and poverty of the village of hand-loom weavers seemed only intensified in the new industrial towns to which the weavers flocked from their deserted hamlets. Manufacturers were doing business under the fiercest and most unregulated competition. Economists were demonstrating their "law of supply and demand" and their "iron law of wages" as capable in themselves of regulating all the conditions and relations of business life. Epidemics raged and depravity prevailed in the new factory centers.

But things were not, in reality, going from bad to worse. The beginnings of a better order had to be based upon two things: first and foremost, the sheer creation of capital; second, the discipline and training of workers. In the first phases, the new modern business period had to be a period of production. There had got to be developed the instrumentalities for the creation of wealth. Until the industrial system had raised up its class of efficient workers and had created its great mass of capital for productive purposes, there could be no supply of cheap goods; and without an abundant and cheap output there could be no possible diffusion of economic benefits; in other words, no marked amelioration of the prevailing poverty.

It required some development of wealth to lift our modern peoples out of a poverty too grinding and too debasing for intellectual or moral progress. It is true that the factory towns, created as they have all been by modern industrial conditions during the past century, brought their distinctive evils. There was overcrowding in ill-built tenement houses; and long hours for women and children in the factories. Yet with these and many other disadvantages, the new industrial system made for discipline and for intelligence, and above all for a new kind of solidarity and for a sense of brotherhood among workers.

In due time the worst evils began to be mitigated, largely through the application of those very methods of organization which had characterized the new kind of industry itself. Thus for men who had applied steam power to manufacturing and had begun to build railroads, it was soon perceived to be a matter not only of sanitary and social service, but of pecuniary profit, to provide water supplies, public illumination, and other conveniences to the crowded city dwellers. Moreover, with the progress of industry and the development of railroads and steam navigation, production and trade took on an ever-increasing volume.

Then the world began to be less poor. There had been no rich men in the modern sense, and of course no such thing as capitalized corporations for production. The richest man in the United States at the time of his death, a little more than a hundred years ago, was George Washington, with his land and his slaves; and so in England and France there were no rich men in the modern sense—that is to say, no men who controlled great masses of productive capital. The men of wealth were those who held landed estates. The chief business of all countries was agriculture. The capitalistic system in industry and trade existed in its rudiments and in limited measure; but all its great achievements were yet to be wrought.

All modern business life, then, is the result of this growth of productive capital, and its application and constant reapplication to the production of wealth. It made its way by virtue of an intense individual initiative and a fierce competitive struggle. But unlovely as were these things, many of their phases were necessary at a certain stage. It was this fierce competition that compelled capital to pay the lowest possible wages in order to market cheap goods. But the same situation stimulated the use, one after another, of new labor-saving inventions in order to increase the per capita productivity. This process was attended by the higher efficiency of the worker and an increase in his earning capacity. As his position began to improve, the worker gained some hope and cheer; and he and his fellows began to organize, with the result that both wages and conditions of labor were steadily improved, and the workman began to attain approximately his share of benefits.

All this is a familiar story, although the depth of its significance is beyond the compass of any living human intelligence. It is easy to say in a glib sentence that the amount of wealth produced every few years nowadays is equal to all the accumulated wealth of all the centuries down to the early part of the nineteenth; but the social meaning of so great a change baffles all attempt at full comprehension.

The competitive system, which had been essential to the launching of this modern period of production, and which had given to it so much of its irresistible momentum, at length brought the economic organization to a point of development where, in some fields of production, it was no longer a benefit. The accumulation of capital had become so large,—and with new inventions the possible output had become so abundant, that it was well nigh impossible to trust to the blind working of demand and supply to regulate things in a beneficial way. It began to dawn on men's minds that a successful period of competitive economic life might lead to a period largely dominated by non-competitive and cooperative principles.

The superior possibilities of this newest régime, along with its many difficulties and perplexities, began to captivate the minds, not merely of theoretical students and onlookers, but, even more, of great masters of industry and productive capital. It began to be seen that in place of blind and fierce competition as a regulator of prices and as an equalizer of supply and demand, there might come to be gradually substituted some more consciously scientific methods of business administration and of the adjustment of production to the needs of the market.

Furthermore, with the development of business on the great scale, capital had become relatively abundant and cheap, while, on the other hand, labor was becoming relatively expensive and exacting. It was evident that the modern system of industry had passed through its earlier period to one of comparative maturity; and that the problem of wealth production was no longer so exclusively the pressing one, but that the problems of distribution were demanding more attention.

How to organize business life on a basis at once stable and efficient; how to see that capital was assured of a normal even though a declining percentage of dividends; while labor should be rewarded according to its capacity and desert,—were problems which took on public rather than private aspects. And when the business world began to face these problems with the consciousness that they were to be met, it had virtually passed over from the lower plane of moral and social responsibility to the higher plane where what the directing minds do or decide is not measured solely by immediate results in money-getting, but also by the test of larger social and public utilities.

Although these conditions are not novel ones, and are therefore not difficult to grasp even when stated in general terms, it is still true that the concrete often helps to make the point appear more pertinent. Take then the railroad business as it is now shaping itself, in comparison with its conditions and methods twenty or thirty years ago. The railroads have always existed by virtue of charters which gave them a quasi-public character, and have always been theoretically subject to certain old principles of English common law under which the public or common carrier, like the innkeeper, performs a function not wholly private in its nature. Nevertheless, in its earlier stages the railroad system of this country was in large part constructed and operated by its projectors with no sense whatever of responsibility for their performance of public functions, but with the idea that they were carrying on their own private business in which interference on the part of the public was to be avoided and resented. They fought the railroad codes of State legislatures in the federal courts; they made oppressive rates to give value to new issues of watered stock; they discriminated in favor of one city and against another; by a system of secret rebates they made different terms with every shipper, thus enabling one merchant or manufacturer to destroy his competitor; and they pursued in general a career at least anti-social in its spirit and false and short-sighted in its principles.

A profound change—would that it were already complete!—is coming about in this great field of transportation business. It is perceived that many of the evils to which I have alluded were incident to the speculative periods of construction and development in a new country. The better leaders in the business of railway administration now see clearly that it is the duty of the railroads to work with and for the public and not against it. The railroads are gradually passing out of the hands of the stockjobbers and speculators, into the control of trained administrators. It is to be remembered that in a country like ours, the largest single branch of organized administration is that of the railroads. We have reached a point where their relations to all the elaborate interests of the community are such that their public character becomes more and more pronounced and evident. It was only the other day that a brilliant railway administrator, Mr. Charles S. Mellen, recently president of the Northern Pacific, and now president of the New York, New Haven & Hartford system, made some statements in an address to the business men of Hartford at a Board of Trade meeting. With much else of the same import, he made the following significant remarks:

"If corporations are to continue to do their work as they are best fitted to, those qualities in their representatives that have resulted in the present prejudice against them must be relegated to the background.

"They must come out into the open and see and be seen. They must take the public into their confidence and ask for what they want and no more, and then be prepared to explain satisfactorily what advantage will accrue to the public if they are given their desires, for they are permitted to exist not that they may make money solely, but that they may effectively serve those from whom they derive their power. Publicity should rule now. Publicity, and not secrecy, will win hereafter, and laws will be construed by their intent and not killed by their letter; otherwise public utilities will be owned and operated by the public which created them, even though the service be less efficient and the result less satisfactory from a financial standpoint."

Mr. Mellen's state of mind is that which ought to prevail among all the managers of corporations which enjoy public franchises and perform functions fundamental to the welfare of the community. There will at times be prejudice and passion on the part of the public, and unfair demands will be made. We shall not see the attainment of ideal conditions in the management or the public relations of any great business corporations in our day. But the time has come when any intelligent and capable young man who chooses to enter the service of a railroad or of some other great corporation may rightly feel that he becomes part of a system whose operation is vital to the public welfare. He may further feel that there is room in such a calling for all his intelligence and for the exercise and growth of all the best sentiments of his moral nature.

In the vast mechanism of modern business the constructive imagination may find its full play; and the desire to be of service to one's fellow men in a spirit reasonably disinterested may find opportunity to satisfy itself every day. Under these circumstances there is no reason why railway administration should not take on the same ethical standards as belong rightly to governmental administration, to educational administration, or to the best professional life.

The same thing is clearly true when one considers nowadays the delicate and important functions of the world of banking and finance. The old-fashioned money-changer and the usurer of earlier periods were regarded as the very antithesis of men engaged in honorable mercantile life, and especially of those who possess a social spirit and the desire to be useful members of the community. But in these days the banks are not merely private money-making institutions, but have public functions that admittedly affect the whole social organism, from the government itself down to the humblest laborer. They must concern themselves about the soundness and the sufficiency of the monetary circulation; they must protect the credit and foster the welfare of honest merchants and manufacturers; they must cooperate in critical times to help one another, and thus to sustain the public and private credit and avert commercial disaster; they must at all hazards protect the savings of the poor. Thus the banks, like the railroads and many other corporate enterprises, are quasi-public affairs, in the conduct of which the public obligation grows ever clearer and stronger.

We are not at heart—in this splendid country of ours—engaged in a mad struggle and race for wealth. We are engaged rather in the greatest effort ever made in the world for the upbuilding of a higher civilization. To avow that this civilization must rest upon a physical and material basis,—that is to say, upon a high development of our productive capacity and upon a constant improvement in our processes of distribution and exchange,—is not, on the other hand, to confess that our civilization is materialistic in its nature or in its aims. I was very glad, the other day, to read the wholesome and understanding words of a distinguished Boston clergyman who is just now coming to New York to take charge of an important parish. He declared that this nation was founded on an ideal, and that the most powerful influences in its life today are working toward noble ideals. The moral and spiritual tone of the country, he asserted, is higher than ever, in spite of the accidents of wealth and poverty. He declared that the great host of men and women who cherish our ideals will continue to stamp idealism upon the minds and hearts of our youth, and that they in turn "will convert wealth to the service of ideals."

Such views are not merely the expressions of a comfortable optimist. They are true to the facts of our current progress. There are vast portions of this country today in which the enterprising business man who can succeed in selling to the farmers an honest and effective commercial fertilizer is the best possible missionary of idealism,—is, in fact, a veritable angel for the spread of sweetness and light. There are regions where the capitalist or the company that will build a cotton mill or some other kind of factory is rescuing whole communities from degradation. It is poverty that has kept the South so backward, and it is poverty alone that explains the illiteracy and the lawlessness not merely of the Kentucky mountains, but of great areas in other States as well. Good schools cannot be supported in regions like those, for the palpable reason that the taxable wealth of an entire school district cannot yield enough to pay the salary of a teacher. But when modern business invades those uplands, utilizes the water-power now wasted, opens the mines, builds cotton factories or foundries, the situation changes almost as if by magic.

There will, indeed, ensue a brief period of disturbance due to changed social conditions,—to women and children in factories, and other things of incidental or serious disadvantage. But, as against a survival of the sort of life that was widely prevalent a century or two ago, all the phenomena of our modern industrial life make their appearance, in full development. The one-room cabin gives place to the little house of several rooms. There is rapid diffusion of those minor comforts and agencies which make for self-respect and personal and family advancement. The advent of capital, that is to say, of taxable property, is speedily followed by the good schoolhouse and the good teacher.

It is instructive to note the transformation that is thus taking place in one county after another of the Carolinas, or Georgia, or others of the Southern States, because the conditions make it possible to witness within a single decade the triumph of those business forces which, while they have even more truly and completely transformed the prosperous parts of America and Europe, have operated more gradually through longer periods, and therefore in a less easily perceived and dramatic fashion.

Our modern ideals have required, not the refinement and the culture of the select few, but the uplifting and progress of the multitude. This could only be possible through a general development of wealth, so vast in comparison with what had previously existed as to constitute the most highly revolutionary fact in the history of human civilization and progress. The man, therefore, who has a clear perception of those laws of mind and of society under which modern economic forces have been set at work, cannot for a moment think that the end and outcome of this modern business system is a new kind of human bondage, "the rich growing richer and the poor growing poorer"; or that it can mean any such thing as the elevation of property at the expense of manhood.

Even if it were a part of my subject to discuss the growth of vast individual fortunes as an incident of this modern development of wealth, which it is not, there would be no time for more than a passing allusion. And in making such an allusion, I might be content to call attention to my earlier dictum, that progress is not upon direct lines, but tangential or zigzag. When the factory appears on the Piedmont slopes of the Appalachian country, it may indeed make a fortune for the missionary of civilization who planted it there. But meanwhile it has given the whole neighborhood its first chance to relate itself to the civilized world. I am content for the present to leave that neighborhood in possession of its opportunities, serenely confident that it will in due time work out its own completer destiny.

When the capitalist has retired from the scene of his exploitation, will the day arrive when the regenerated neighborhood will own that factory, and others, too, for itself? Very likely. In any case, the neighborhood has been emancipated from its worst disadvantages.

In short, I have little doubt but that the further progress of our civilization will give effect to certain economic laws and tendencies, and to certain social rules and principles, that will make for a higher measure of equality in the distribution of realized wealth. Meanwhile wherever a practical step can be taken to remedy an evil, let us do what we can to promote that step. Let us recognize the already great possibilities for useful participation in the social and public life that belong to an honorable business career.

From the standpoint of the intellectual interest of the young man going into business, let it be borne in mind that there are scientific principles underlying every branch of trade or commerce or industry, and that there is almost, if not quite, as much room for the delightful play of the faculty of imagination in the successful conduct of a soap business as in writing poetry or in making statuary groups for world's fairs. The cultivation of public spirit in the broad sense, and the determination to be an all-round good and efficient citizen and member of the community, will often help a man amazingly to discern the opportunities for usefulness that lie in the direct line of his business work. The more thoroughly he studies underlying principles—whether of a technical sort as related to his own trade, or of a general sort having to do with the organization and general methods of commerce—the less likely he will be to take narrow and anti-social views of business life. The high development of his intelligence in relation to his own work will show him the value in his business—as in all else in life—of the standard thing, the genuine thing, the thing that will bear the test as contrasted with the shoddy, or the inferior, or the spurious.

Our technological schools, our colleges of mechanic arts, our institutes of agriculture and their related experiment stations,—these are all teaching us many valuable object-lessons regarding the way in which the wealth of the individual and that of the community can both, at the same time, be advanced by scientific methods. Thus it is coming about that business life is ever more ready to welcome the most highly trained kinds of intelligence, inasmuch as it is perceived that specialized knowledge is henceforth to be the most valuable commodity that a man can possess.

I have already said that the delicate problems of distribution must be faced ever more frankly and liberally by the modern business world. Thus, those who control capital, or administer capitalized enterprises, cannot afford any longer to be without a knowledge of the history and significance of the labor movement. We should not have had the desperate struggle between anthracite coal corporations and the miners in Pennsylvania, a year or so ago, if there had been a full understanding on the part of the capitalists of the honorable and valuable nature of trade agreements, and particularly of the history of the relations of capital and labor in the bituminous coal districts of the United States. I am speaking now from the standpoint of the business man. There is much to be said, doubtless, in respect to the shortcomings and the sometimes fatuous and even suicidal methods of the labor organizations. But for the modern business man who cares to take his place influentially in commerce, in social life, and as a man among men in his city or his commonwealth, it is no longer justifiable to be unfamiliar with the labor question in its economics and its history.

Herein lies one great service that the university can perform (and our best colleges and universities are today performing it with marked intelligence and ability), the service, namely, of providing very liberal courses for young men who expect to go into business, in the general science of economics, in the history of modern economic progress, in the development of the wage system, in the history and methods of organized labor, and in very much else that helps to place the life of a practical man of business affairs upon a broad and liberal basis. In the early days of our history it was the especial function of the college to train young men for the ministry. In a somewhat later period it was notably true of institutions like Yale and Princeton that their training seemed to fit many men for the law and for statecraft. We had, you see, passed from that theocratic phase of colonial New England life to the political constructive period of our young republic.

But we have been passing on until we have emerged in a great and transcendent period of commercial expansion and scientific discovery and application. It is a hopeful sign, therefore, that our universities are finding out and admitting the demand that present-day conditions impose, and are training many men in the pursuit of modern science, while they are training many others in the understanding of the application of social and economic principles to modern life. All this they are doing and can well do without ignoring the value of the older forms of scholarship and culture.

But I have a few remarks to make also upon the ethical relations of the business world of today toward the political world; that is to say, toward organized government, whether in its sovereign or in its subordinate forms. We cannot take too high a ground in proclaiming the value, for the present, at least, of the political organization of society. I should like to dwell upon this point, but I must merely state it. If the State: *i.e.*, the political form of social organization, is valuable,—it stands to reason that it must be respected and maintained at its best. It is also obvious that it will have a higher or a lower character and efficiency, according to the attitude toward it taken by one or another of the dominant factors that make up the complex body politic.

Thus, for example, it is the feeling of men in control of the political organization in France today that the Church, as a great factor in the social structure of the nation, is essentially hostile to the spirit and purposes of a liberal republic. Hence a great disturbance of various relationships. I do not cite that instance to express even the shade of an opinion. My point is that if the political organization of society is desirable and to be maintained, it is a fortunate thing when one finds the dominant forces of society rendering loyal and faithful support to the laws and institutions of government and recognizing without reserve the sovereignty of the State. Yet in our own country there is a widespread feeling that many of the most potent forces and agencies in our business life are not wholly patriotic, in that they are not willing in practice to recognize the necessity of the domination of government and of law. I do not believe that this is permanently and generally true. It would constitute a great danger if it were a fixed or a growing tendency.

As matters stand, however, every one must admit that there is an element of danger that lies in the very fact that as a nation we are in a condition of peace, content, and prosperity, and do not find our political institutions irksome. The danger consists in this: that under such circumstances the rewards of business and professional life are for the most part so much more certain and satisfactory than those which come from the precarious pursuit of politics, that public interests have a tendency to suffer from being in weak hands, while private interests have a tendency to assert themselves unduly, from being in the hands of men of superior force. Thus it happens that it is often difficult for the State to maintain that dignity, that mastery, that high position, as the impartial arbiter and dispenser of justice, which it is now even more necessary than ever that it should maintain, in order that the whole social organization should keep a true harmony and a safe balance.

At present, the State is largely concerned with the maintenance of conditions under which the economic and business life may operate equally and prosperously. The State in one sense is the master of the people. In another sense it is merely their creature and their agent for such purposes as they choose to assign it. Is the State, then, to absorb the industrial functions, and are we to develop into a socialistic commonwealth? Or, shall the political democracy and the coöperative organization of business life go on side by side, related at many points but in the main distinct from each other? Whatever the relation of the State to industry may be destined to become in the distant future, we may be sure that there will be no rash upheavals, no harmful socialistic experiments, if the potent business world clearly sees how necessary to its own salvation it is that the State shall be maintained upon a high plane of dignity and honor, and that the official dispensation of justice, as well as the official administration of the laws, shall be prompt, just and impartial.

There is no higher duty, therefore, incumbent upon the business man of today than to bear his part in promoting and maintaining the purity of political life. The modern business man should regard good government as one of the vital conditions of the best economic progress. Yet scores of instances are at hand that show to what a painful extent certain business interests again and again, for purposes of immediate advantage,—to secure a franchise, to escape a tax, or to procure some improper favor or advantage at the hands of those in political authority,—have employed corrupt methods and thus stained the fair escutcheon of American business honor, while breaking down the one most indispensable condition of general business progress,—namely, honest and efficient free government.

I will not dwell upon these things. It is enough to say that they are things the modern business man must have upon his conscience. For, if such offenses come by way of the business world, their remedies must also come, and indeed can only come, by that same path. In our municipal life, for example, it is the aroused interest and zeal of the best business community for better government and better conditions that can alone produce important results. Happily, all over the country we find chambers of commerce, boards of trade, merchants' associations, and other bodies of men of practical business affairs, taking their stand for the transaction of public business upon high standards of character and efficiency. I have no doubt or fears as to what the result will be. All of our large cities are themselves purely the creations of modern industrial, commercial, and transportation conditions. And I hold that these very forces of industrial and commercial life that have created the problems by bringing together great masses of people in crowded communities, must and can in turn solve the problems by the application to municipal government of the scientific and intelligent principles which belong to the best phases of business life.

All of this relates to my subject; but I must pass it by with a mere statement or two. It belongs to the developed constructive imagination and to the trained ethical sense of the modern business man to perfect the transit systems, to improve the housing conditions, to assure cheap sanitary water supplies, cheap illumination, and, above all, due provision for universal education, parks, museums, and opportunities for recreation,—in short, all possible improvements of environment that can make life in our cities not merely endurable but beneficial for the people. Here, then, is furnished a great field for the definite and conscious aspirations of the successful man of business. Here lies a great many-sided work for social and moral as well as physical and material progress which the business man, in the quality of good citizen and man of public spirit, is fitted better than anyone else to accomplish.

The intelligent young man who holds before himself ideals of usefulness that extend to such projects as these, may be sure that the modern conditions of life will bring him great opportunities, and he may feel that he is thus lifting his business career up to the plane of idealism that has, in the past, been reserved for a few exclusive professions. Partly through his own endeavors,—largely through association in commercial or other organizations with his neighbors,—he may help to accomplish for the benefit of all his fellow men of a great community one step after another in the direction of public works that will meet the needs of a high civilization.

Some of the most useful men, as well as the most unselfish and devoted, with whom I come in contact are successful business men of large affairs. They are modest and unassuming; simple and direct in their methods; wide as the world in their sympathies; lofty as the stars in their aspirations for human progress; sagacious beyond other classes of men, and respected to the point of veneration by those who know them well, because they are men of deeds rather than of words, who make good their professions from day to day. Business has not so narrowed them, nor has devotion to philanthropic ends or public reforms so distorted their mental visions, that they are not able to enjoy what is good in life, whether books, music, pictures, the companionship of friends, or the restful contact with nature in field or forest.

The lives of such men are dominated by certain fixed ethical standards. Given such moral landmarks, the remarkable conditions and unequaled opportunities of modern business life will promote the frequent development of men of this kind, with their breadth of view and strength of mind and character. It is the positive and aggressive attitude toward life, the ethics of action, rather than the ethics of negation, that must control the modern business world, and that may make our modern business man the most potent factor for good in this, his own, industrial period.

THE ART OF MONEY GETTING
OR
GOLDEN RULES FOR MAKING MONEY
BY P. T. BARNUM

In the United States, where we have more land than people, it is not at all difficult for persons in good health to make money. In this comparatively new field there are so many avenues of success open, so many vocations which are not crowded, that any person of either sex who is willing, at least for the time being, to engage in any respectable occupation that offers, may find lucrative employment.

Those who really desire to attain an independence, have only to set their minds upon it, and adopt the proper means, as they do in regard to any other object which they wish to accomplish, and the thing is easily done. But however easy it may be found to make money, I have no doubt many of my hearers will agree it is the most difficult thing in the world to keep it. The road to wealth is, as Dr. Franklin truly says, "as plain as the road to the mill." It consists simply in expending less than we earn; that seems to be a very simple problem. Mr. Micawber, one of those happy creations of the genial Dickens, puts the case in a strong light when he says that to have annual income of twenty pounds per annum, and spend twenty pounds and sixpence, is to be the most miserable of men; whereas, to have an income of only twenty pounds, and spend but nineteen pounds and sixpence is to be the happiest of mortals. Many of my readers may say, "we understand this: this is economy, and we know economy is wealth; we know we can't eat our cake and keep it also." Yet I beg to say that perhaps more cases of failure arise from mistakes on this point than almost any other. The fact is, many people think they understand economy when they really do not.

True economy is misapprehended, and people go through life without properly comprehending what that principle is. One says, "I have an income of so much, and here is my neighbor who has the same; yet every year he gets something ahead and I fall short; why is it? I know all about economy." He thinks he does, but he does not. There are men who think that economy consists in saving cheese-parings and candle-ends, in cutting off two pence from the laundress' bill and doing all sorts of little, mean, dirty things. Economy is not meanness. The misfortune is, also, that this class of persons let their economy apply in only one direction. They fancy they are so wonderfully economical in saving a half-penny where they ought to spend twopence, that they think they can afford to squander in other directions. A few years ago, before kerosene oil was discovered or thought of, one might stop overnight at almost any farmer's house in the agricultural districts and get a very good supper, but after supper he might attempt to read in the sitting-room, and would find it impossible with the inefficient light of one candle. The hostess, seeing his dilemma, would say: "It is rather difficult to read here evenings; the proverb says 'you must have a ship at sea in order to be able to burn two candles at once;' we never have an extra candle except on extra occasions." These extra occasions occur, perhaps, twice a year. In this way the good woman saves five, six, or ten dollars in that time: but the information which might be derived from having the extra light would, of course, far outweigh a ton of candles.

But the trouble does not end here. Feeling that she is so economical in tallow candies, she thinks she can afford to go frequently to the village and spend twenty or thirty dollars for ribbons and furbelows, many of which are not necessary. This false connote may frequently be seen in men of business, and in those instances it often runs to writing-paper. You find good businessmen who save all the old envelopes and scraps, and would not tear a new sheet of paper, if they could avoid it, for the world. This is all very well; they may in this way save five or ten dollars a year, but being so economical (only in note paper), they think they can afford to waste time; to have expensive parties, and to drive their carriages. This is an illustration of Dr. Franklin's "saving at the spigot and wasting at the bung-hole;" "penny wise and pound foolish." Punch in speaking of this "one idea" class of people says "they are like the man who bought a penny herring for his family's dinner and then hired a coach and four to take it home." I never knew a man to succeed by practising this kind of economy.

True economy consists in always making the income exceed the out-go. Wear the old clothes a little longer if necessary; dispense with the new pair of gloves; mend the old dress: live on plainer food if need be; so that, under all circumstances, unless some unforeseen accident occurs, there will be a margin in favor of the income. A penny here, and a dollar there, placed at interest, goes on accumulating, and in this way the desired result is attained.

It requires some training, perhaps, to accomplish this economy, but when once used to it, you will find there is more satisfaction in rational saving than in irrational spending. Here is a recipe which I recommend: I have found it to work an excellent cure for extravagance, and especially for mistaken economy: When you find that you have no surplus at the end of the year, and yet have a good income, I advise you to take a few sheets of paper and form them into a book and mark down every item of expenditure. Post it every day or week in two columns, one headed "necessaries" or even "comforts", and the other headed "luxuries," and you will find that the latter column will be double, treble, and frequently ten times greater than the former. The real comforts of life cost but a small portion of what most of us can earn. Dr. Franklin says "it is the eyes of others and not our own eyes which ruin us. If all the world were blind except myself I should not care for fine clothes or furniture." It is the fear of what Mrs. Grundy may say that keeps the noses of many worthy families to the grindstone. In America many persons like to repeat "we are all free and equal," but it is a great mistake in more senses than one.

That we are born "free and equal" is a glorious truth in one sense, yet we are not all born equally rich, and we never shall be. One may say; "there is a man who has an income of fifty thousand dollars per annum, while I have but one thousand dollars; I knew that fellow when he was poor like myself; now he is rich and thinks he is better than I am; I will show him that I am as good as he is; I will go and buy a horse and buggy; no, I cannot do that, but I will go and hire one and ride this afternoon on the same road that he does, and thus prove to him that I am as good as he is."

My friend, you need not take that trouble; you can easily prove that you are "as good as he is;" you have only to behave as well as he does; but you cannot make anybody believe that you are rich as he is. Besides, if you put on these "airs," add waste your time and spend your money, your poor wife will be obliged to scrub her fingers off at home, and buy her tea two ounces at a time, and everything else in proportion, in order that you may keep up "appearances," and, after all, deceive nobody. On the other hand, Mrs. Smith may say that her next-door neighbor married Johnson for his money, and "everybody says so." She has a nice one-thousand dollar camel's hair shawl, and she will make Smith get her an imitation one, and she will sit in a pew right next to her neighbor in church, in order to prove that she is her equal.

My good woman, you will not get ahead in the world, if your vanity and envy thus take the lead. In this country, where we believe the majority ought to rule, we ignore that principle in regard to fashion, and let a handful of people, calling themselves the aristocracy, run up a false standard of perfection, and in endeavoring to rise to that standard, we constantly keep ourselves poor; all the time digging away for the sake of outside appearances. How much wiser to be a "law unto ourselves" and say, "we will regulate our out-go by our income, and lay up something for a rainy day." People ought to be as sensible on the subject of money-getting as on any other subject. Like causes produces like effects. You cannot accumulate a fortune by taking the road that leads to poverty. It needs no prophet to tell us that those who live fully up to their means, without any thought of a reverse in this life, can never attain a pecuniary independence.

Men and women accustomed to gratify every whim and caprice, will find it hard, at first, to cut down their various unnecessary expenses, and will feel it a great self-denial to live in a smaller house than they have been accustomed to, with less expensive furniture, less company, less costly clothing, fewer servants, a less number of balls, parties, theater-goings, carriage-ridings, pleasure excursions, cigar-smokings, liquor-drinkings, and other extravagances; but, after all, if they will try the plan of laying by a "nest-egg," or, in other words, a small sum of money, at interest or judiciously invested in land, they will be surprised at the pleasure to be derived from constantly adding to their little "pile," as well as from all the economical habits which are engendered by this course.

The old suit of clothes, and the old bonnet and dress, will answer for another season; the Croton or spring water taste better than champagne; a cold bath and a brisk walk will prove more exhilarating than a ride in the finest coach; a social chat, an evening's reading in the family circle, or an hour's play of "hunt the slipper" and "blind man's buff" will be far more pleasant than a fifty or five hundred dollar party, when the reflection on the difference in cost is indulged in by those who begin to know the pleasures of saving. Thousands of men are kept poor, and tens of thousands are made so after they have acquired quite sufficient to support them well through life, in consequence of laying their plans of living on too broad a platform. Some families expend twenty thousand dollars per annum, and some much more, and would scarcely know how to live on less, while others secure more solid enjoyment frequently on a twentieth part of that amount. Prosperity is a more severe ordeal than adversity, especially sudden prosperity. "Easy come, easy go," is an old and true proverb. A spirit of pride and vanity, when permitted to have full sway, is the undying canker-worm which gnaws the very vitals of a man's worldly possessions, let them be small or great, hundreds, or millions. Many persons, as they begin to prosper, immediately expand their ideas and commence expending for luxuries, until in a short time their expenses swallow up their income, and they become ruined in their ridiculous attempts to keep up appearances, and make a "sensation."

I know a gentleman of fortune who says, that when he first began to prosper, his wife would have a new and elegant sofa. "That sofa," he says, "cost me thirty thousand dollars!" When the sofa reached the house, it was found necessary to get chairs to match; then side-boards, carpets and tables "to correspond" with them, and so on through the entire stock of furniture; when at last it was found that the house itself was quite too small and old-fashioned for the furniture, and a new one was built to correspond with the new purchases; "thus," added my friend, "summing up an outlay of thirty thousand dollars, caused by that single sofa, and saddling on me, in the shape of servants, equipage, and the necessary expenses attendant upon keeping up a fine 'establishment,' a yearly outlay of eleven thousand dollars, and a tight pinch at that: whereas, ten years ago, we lived with much more real comfort, because with much less care, on as many hundreds. The truth is," he continued, "that sofa would have brought me to inevitable bankruptcy, had not a most unexampled title to prosperity kept me above it, and had I not checked the natural desire to 'cut a dash'."

The foundation of success in life is good health: that is the substratum fortune; it is also the basis of happiness. A person cannot accumulate a fortune very well when he is sick. He has no ambition; no incentive; no force. Of course, there are those who have bad health and cannot help it: you cannot expect that such persons can accumulate wealth, but there are a great many in poor health who need not be so.

If, then, sound health is the foundation of success and happiness in life, how important it is that we should study the laws of health, which is but another expression for the laws of nature! The nearer we keep to the laws of nature, the nearer we are to good health, and yet how many persons there are who pay no attention to natural laws, but absolutely transgress them, even against their own natural inclination. We ought to know that the "sin of ignorance" is never winked at in regard to the violation of nature's laws; their infraction always brings the penalty. A child may thrust its finger into the flames without knowing it will burn, and so suffers, repentance, even, will not stop the smart. Many of our ancestors knew very little about the principle of ventilation. They did not know much about oxygen, whatever other "gin" they might have been acquainted with; and consequently they built their houses with little seven-by-nine feet bedrooms, and these good old pious Puritans would lock themselves up in one of these cells, say their prayers and go to bed. In the morning they would devoutly return thanks for the "preservation of their lives," during the night, and nobody had better reason to be thankful. Probably some big crack in the window, or in the door, let in a little fresh air, and thus saved them.

Many persons knowingly violate the laws of nature against their better impulses, for the sake of fashion. For instance, there is one thing that nothing living except a vile worm ever naturally loved, and that is tobacco; yet how many persons there are who deliberately train an unnatural appetite, and overcome this implanted aversion for tobacco, to such a degree that they get to love it. They have got hold of a poisonous, filthy weed, or rather that takes a firm hold of them. Here are married men who run about spitting tobacco juice on the carpet and floors, and sometimes even upon their wives besides. They do not kick their wives out of doors like drunken men, but their wives, I have no doubt, often wish they were outside of the house. Another perilous feature is that this artificial appetite, like jealousy, "grows by what it feeds on;" when you love that which is unnatural, a stronger appetite is created for the hurtful thing than the natural desire for what is harmless. There is an old proverb which says that "habit is second nature," but an artificial habit is stronger than nature. Take for instance, an old tobacco-chewer; his love for the "quid" is stronger than his love for any particular kind of food. He can give up roast beef easier than give up the weed.

Young lads regret that they are not men; they would like to go to bed boys and wake up men; and to accomplish this they copy the bad habits of their seniors. Little Tommy and Johnny see their fathers or uncles smoke a pipe, and they say, "If I could only do that, I would be a man too; uncle John has gone out and left his pipe of tobacco, let us try it." They take a match and light it, and then puff away. "We will learn to smoke; do you like it Johnny?" That lad dolefully replies: "Not very much; it tastes bitter;" by and by he grows pale, but he persists and he soon offers up a sacrifice on the altar of fashion; but the boys stick to it and persevere until at last they conquer their natural appetites and become the victims of acquired tastes.

I speak "by the book," for I have noticed its effects on myself, having gone so far as to smoke ten or fifteen cigars a day; although I have not used the weed during the last fourteen years, and never shall again. The more a man smokes, the more he craves smoking; the last cigar smoked simply excites the desire for another, and so on incessantly.

Take the tobacco-chewer. In the morning, when he gets up, he puts a quid in his mouth and keeps it there all day, never taking it out except to exchange it for a fresh one, or when he is going to eat; oh! yes, at intervals during the day and evening, many a chewer takes out the quid and holds it in his hand long enough to take a drink, and then pop it goes back again. This simply proves that the appetite for rum is even stronger than that for tobacco. When the tobacco-chewer goes to your country seat and you show him your grapery and fruit house, and the beauties of your garden, when you offer him some fresh, ripe fruit, and say, "My friend, I have got here the most delicious apples, and pears, and peaches, and apricots; I have imported them from Spain, France and Italy—just see those luscious grapes; there is nothing more delicious nor more healthy than ripe fruit, so help yourself; I want to see you delight yourself with these things;" he will roll the dear quid under his tongue and answer, "No, I thank you, I have got tobacco in my mouth." His palate has become narcotized by the noxious weed, and he has lost, in a great measure, the delicate and enviable taste for fruits. This shows what expensive, useless and injurious habits men will get into. I speak from experience. I have smoked until I trembled like an aspen leaf, the blood rushed to my head, and I had a palpitation of the heart which I thought was heart disease, till I was almost killed with fright. When I consulted my physician, he said "break off tobacco using." I was not only injuring my health and spending a great deal of money, but I was setting a bad example. I obeyed his counsel. No young man in the world ever looked so beautiful, as he thought he did, behind a fifteen cent cigar or a meerschaum!

These remarks apply with tenfold force to the use of intoxicating drinks. To make money, requires a clear brain. A man has got to see that two and two make four; he must lay all his plans with reflection and forethought, and closely examine all the details and the ins and outs of business. As no man can succeed in business unless he has a brain to enable him to lay his plans, and reason to guide him in their execution, so, no matter how bountifully a man may be blessed with intelligence, if the brain is muddled, and his judgment warped by intoxicating drinks, it is impossible for him to carry on business successfully. How many good opportunities have passed, never to return, while a man was sipping a "social glass," with his friend! How many foolish bargains have been made under the influence of the "nervine," which temporarily makes its victim think he is rich. How many important chances have been put off until to-morrow, and then forever, because the wine cup has thrown the system into a state of lassitude, neutralizing the energies so essential to success in business. Verily, "wine is a mocker." The use of intoxicating drinks as a beverage, is as much an infatuation, as is the smoking of opium by the Chinese, and the former is quite as destructive to the success of the business man as the latter. It is an unmitigated evil, utterly indefensible in the light of philosophy; religion or good sense. It is the parent of nearly every other evil in our country.

DON'T MISTAKE YOUR VOCATION

The safest plan, and the one most sure of success for the young man starting in life, is to select the vocation which is most congenial to his tastes. Parents and guardians are often quite too negligent in regard to this. It very common for a father to say, for example: "I have five boys. I will make Billy a clergyman; John a lawyer; Tom a doctor, and Dick a farmer." He then goes into town and looks about to see what he will do with Sammy. He returns home and says "Sammy, I see watch-making is a nice genteel business; I think I will make you a goldsmith." He does this, regardless of Sam's natural inclinations, or genius.

We are all, no doubt, born for a wise purpose. There is as much diversity in our brains as in our countenances. Some are born natural mechanics, while some have great aversion to machinery. Let a dozen boys of ten years get together, and you will soon observe two or three are "whittling" out some ingenious device; working with locks or complicated machinery. When they were but five years old, their father could find no toy to please them like a puzzle. They are natural mechanics; but the other eight or nine boys have different aptitudes. I belong to the latter class; I never had the slightest love for mechanism; on the contrary, I have a sort of abhorrence for complicated machinery. I never had ingenuity enough to whittle a cider tap so it would not leak. I never could make a pen that I could write with, or understand the principle of a steam engine. If a man was to take such a boy as I was, and attempt to make a watchmaker of him, the boy might, after an apprenticeship of five or seven years, be able to take apart and put together a watch; but all through life he would be working up hill and seizing every excuse for leaving his work and idling away his time. Watchmaking is repulsive to him.

Unless a man enters upon the vocation intended for him by nature, and best suited to his peculiar genius, he cannot succeed. I am glad to believe that the majority of persons do find their right vocation. Yet we see many who have mistaken their calling, from the blacksmith up (or down) to the clergyman. You will see, for instance, that extraordinary linguist the "learned blacksmith," who ought to have been a teacher of languages; and you may have seen lawyers, doctors and clergymen who were better fitted by nature for the anvil or the lapstone.

SELECT THE RIGHT LOCATION

After securing the right vocation, you must be careful to select the proper location. You may have been cut out for a hotel keeper, and they say it requires a genius to "know how to keep a hotel." You might conduct a hotel like clock-work, and provide satisfactorily for five hundred guests every day; yet, if you should locate your house in a small village where there is no railroad communication or public travel, the location would be your ruin. It is equally important that you do not commence business where there are already enough to meet all demands in the same occupation. I remember a case which illustrates this subject. When I was in London in 1858, I was passing down Holborn with an English friend and came to the "penny shows." They had immense cartoons outside, portraying the wonderful curiosities to be seen "all for a penny." Being a little in the "show line" myself, I said "let us go in here." We soon found ourselves in the presence of the illustrious showman, and he proved to be the sharpest man in that line I had ever met. He told us some extraordinary stories in reference to his bearded ladies, his Albinos, and his Armadillos, which we could hardly believe, but thought it "better to believe it than look after the proof." He finally begged to call our attention to some wax statuary, and showed us a lot of the dirtiest and filthiest wax figures imaginable. They looked as if they had not seen water since the Deluge.

"What is there so wonderful about your statuary?" I asked.

"I beg you not to speak so satirically," he replied, "Sir, these are not Madam Tussaud's wax figures, all covered with gilt and tinsel and imitation diamonds, and copied from engravings and photographs. Mine, sir, were taken from life. Whenever you look upon one of those figures, you may consider that you are looking upon the living individual."

Glancing casually at them, I saw one labeled "Henry VIII," and feeling a little curious upon seeing that it looked like Calvin Edson, the living skeleton, I said: "Do you call that 'Henry the Eighth?'" He replied, "Certainly; sir; it was taken from life at Hampton Court, by special order of his majesty; on such a day."

He would have given the hour of the day if I had resisted; I said, "Everybody knows that 'Henry VIII.' was a great stout old king, and that figure is lean and lank; what do you say to that?"

"Why," he replied, "you would be lean and lank yourself if you sat there as long as he has."

There was no resisting such arguments. I said to my English friend, "Let us go out; do not tell him who I am; I show the white feather; he beats me."

He followed us to the door, and seeing the rabble in the street, he called out, "ladies and gentlemen, I beg to draw your attention to the respectable character of my visitors," pointing to us as we walked away. I called upon him a couple of days afterwards; told him who I was, and said:

"My friend, you are an excellent showman, but you have selected a bad location."

He replied, "This is true, sir; I feel that all my talents are thrown away; but what can I do?"

"You can go to America," I replied. "You can give full play to your faculties over there; you will find plenty of elbowroom in America; I will engage you for two years; after that you will be able to go on your own account."

He accepted my offer and remained two years in my New York Museum. He then went to New Orleans and carried on a traveling show business during the summer. To-day he is worth sixty thousand dollars, simply because he selected the right vocation and also secured the proper location. The old proverb says, "Three removes are as bad as a fire," but when a man is in the fire, it matters but little how soon or how often he removes.

AVOID DEBT

Young men starting in life should avoid running into debt. There is scarcely anything that drags a person down like debt. It is a slavish position to get in, yet we find many a young man, hardly out of his "teens," running in debt. He meets a chum and says, "Look at this: I have got trusted for a new suit of clothes." He seems to look upon the clothes as so much given to him; well, it frequently is so, but, if he succeeds in paying and then gets trusted again, he is adopting a habit which will keep him in poverty through life. Debt robs a man of his self-respect, and makes him almost despise himself. Grunting and groaning and working for what he has eaten up or worn out, and now when he is called upon to pay up, he has nothing to show for his money; this is properly termed "working for a dead horse." I do not speak of merchants buying and selling on credit, or of those who buy on credit in order to turn the purchase to a profit. The old Quaker said to his farmer son, "John, never get trusted; but if thee gets trusted for anything, let it be for 'manure,' because that will help thee pay it back again."

Mr. Beecher advised young men to get in debt if they could to a small amount in the purchase of land, in the country districts. "If a young man," he says, "will only get in debt for some land and then get married, these two things will keep him straight, or nothing will." This may be safe to a limited extent, but getting in debt for what you eat and drink and wear is to be avoided. Some families have a foolish habit of getting credit at "the stores," and thus frequently purchase many things which might have been dispensed with.

It is all very well to say; "I have got trusted for sixty days, and if I don't have the money the creditor will think nothing about it." There is no class of people in the world, who have such good memories as creditors. When the sixty days run out, you will have to pay. If you do not pay, you will break your promise, and probably resort to a falsehood. You may make some excuse or get in debt elsewhere to pay it, but that only involves you the deeper.

A good-looking, lazy young fellow, was the apprentice boy, Horatio. His employer said, "Horatio, did you ever see a snail?" "I—think—I—have," he drawled out. "You must have met him then, for I am sure you never overtook one," said the "boss." Your creditor will meet you or overtake you and say, "Now, my young friend, you agreed to pay me; you have not done it, you must give me your note." You give the note on interest and it commences working against you; "it is a dead horse." The creditor goes to bed at night and wakes up in the morning better off than when he retired to bed, because his interest has increased during the night, but you grow poorer while you are sleeping, for the interest is accumulating against you.

Money is in some respects like fire; it is a very excellent servant but a terrible master. When you have it mastering you; when interest is constantly piling up against you, it will keep you down in the worst kind of slavery. But let money work for you, and you have the most devoted servant in the world. It is no "eye-servant." There is nothing animate or inanimate that will work so faithfully as money when placed at interest, well secured. It works night and day, and in wet or dry weather.

I was born in the blue-law State of Connecticut, where the old Puritans had laws so rigid that it was said, "they fined a man for kissing his wife on Sunday." Yet these rich old Puritans would have thousands of dollars at interest, and on Saturday night would be worth a certain amount; on Sunday they would go to church and perform all the duties of a Christian. On waking up on Monday morning, they would find themselves considerably richer than the Saturday night previous, simply because their money placed at interest had worked faithfully for them all day Sunday, according to law!

Do not let it work against you; if you do there is no chance for success in life so far as money is concerned. John Randolph, the eccentric Virginian, once exclaimed in Congress, "Mr. Speaker, I have discovered the philosopher's stone: pay as you go." This is, indeed, nearer to the philosopher's stone than any alchemist has ever yet arrived.

PERSEVERE

When a man is in the right path, he must persevere. I speak of this because there are some persons who are "born tired;" naturally lazy and possessing no self-reliance and no perseverance. But they can cultivate these qualities, as Davy Crockett said: "This thing remember, when I am dead: Be sure you are right, then go ahead."

It is this go-aheaditiveness, this determination not to let the "horrors" or the "blues" take possession of you, so as to make you relax your energies in the struggle for independence, which you must cultivate.

How many have almost reached the goal of their ambition, but, losing faith in themselves, have relaxed their energies, and the golden prize has been lost forever.

It is, no doubt, often true, as Shakespeare says: "There is a tide in the affairs of men, Which, taken at the flood, leads on to fortune."

If you hesitate, some bolder hand will stretch out before you and get the prize. Remember the proverb of Solomon: "He becometh poor that dealeth with a slack hand; but the hand of the diligent maketh rich."

Perseverance is sometimes but another word for self-reliance. Many persons naturally look on the dark side of life, and borrow trouble. They are born so. Then they ask for advice, and they will be governed by one wind and blown by another, and cannot rely upon themselves. Until you can get so that you can rely upon yourself, you need not expect to succeed.

I have known men, personally, who have met with pecuniary reverses, and absolutely committed suicide, because they thought they could never overcome their misfortune. But I have known others who have met more serious financial difficulties, and have bridged them over by simple perseverance, aided by a firm belief that they were doing justly, and that Providence would "overcome evil with good." You will see this illustrated in any sphere of life.

Take two generals; both understand military tactics, both educated at West Point, if you please, both equally gifted; yet one, having this principle of perseverance, and the other lacking it, the former will succeed in his profession, while the latter will fail. One may hear the cry, "the enemy are coming, and they have got cannon."

"Got cannon?" says the hesitating general.

"Yes."

"Then halt every man."

He wants time to reflect; his hesitation is his ruin; the enemy passes unmolested, or overwhelms him; while on the other hand, the general of pluck, perseverance and self-reliance, goes into battle with a will, and, amid the clash of arms, the booming of cannon, the shrieks of the wounded, and the moans of the dying, you will see this man persevering, going on, cutting and slashing his way through with unwavering determination, inspiring his soldiers to deeds of fortitude, valor, and triumph.

WHATEVER YOU DO, DO IT WITH ALL YOUR MIGHT

Work at it, if necessary, early and late, in season and out of season, not leaving a stone unturned, and never deferring for a single hour that which can be done just as well now. The old proverb is full of truth and meaning, "Whatever is worth doing at all, is worth doing well." Many a man acquires a fortune by doing his business thoroughly, while his neighbor remains poor for life, because he only half does it. Ambition, energy, industry, perseverance, are indispensable requisites for success in business.

Fortune always favors the brave, and never helps a man who does not help himself. It won't do to spend your time like Mr. Micawber, in waiting for something to "turn up." To such men one of two things usually "turns up:" the poorhouse or the jail; for idleness breeds bad habits, and clothes a man in rags. The poor spendthrift vagabond says to a rich man:

"I have discovered there is enough money in the world for all of us, if it was equally divided; this must be done, and we shall all be happy together."

"But," was the response, "if everybody was like you, it would be spent in two months, and what would you do then?"

"Oh! divide again; keep dividing, of course!"

I was recently reading in a London paper an account of a like philosophic pauper who was kicked out of a cheap boarding-house because he could not pay his bill, but he had a roll of papers sticking out of his coat pocket, which, upon examination, proved to be his plan for paying off the national debt of England without the aid of a penny. People have got to do as Cromwell said: "not only trust in Providence, but keep the powder dry." Do your part of the work, or you cannot succeed. Mahomet, one night, while encamping in the desert, overheard one of his fatigued followers remark: "I will loose my camel, and trust it to God!" "No, no, not so," said the prophet, "tie thy camel, and trust it to God!" Do all you can for yourselves, and then trust to Providence, or luck, or whatever you please to call it, for the rest.

DEPEND UPON YOUR OWN PERSONAL EXERTIONS

The eye of the employer is often worth more than the hands of a dozen employees. In the nature of things, an agent cannot be so faithful to his employer as to himself. Many who are employers will call to mind instances where the best employees have overlooked important points which could not have escaped their own observation as a proprietor. No man has a right to expect to succeed in life unless he understands his business, and nobody can understand his business thoroughly unless he learns it by personal application and experience. A man may be a manufacturer: he has got to learn the many details of his business personally; he will learn something every day, and he will find he will make mistakes nearly every day. And these very mistakes are helps to him in the way of experiences if he but heeds them. He will be like the Yankee tin-peddler, who, having been cheated as to quality in the purchase of his merchandise, said: "All right, there's a little information to be gained every day; I will never be cheated in that way again." Thus a man buys his experience, and it is the best kind if not purchased at too dear a rate.

I hold that every man should, like Cuvier, the French naturalist, thoroughly know his business. So proficient was he in the study of natural history, that you might bring to him the bone, or even a section of a bone of an animal which he had never seen described, and, reasoning from analogy, he would be able to draw a picture of the object from which the bone had been taken. On one occasion his students attempted to deceive him. They rolled one of their number in a cow skin and put him under the professor's table as a new specimen. When the philosopher came into the room, some of the students asked him what animal it was. Suddenly the animal said "I am the devil and I am going to eat you." It was but natural that Cuvier should desire to classify this creature, and examining it intently, he said:

"Divided hoof; graminivorous! It cannot be done."

He knew that an animal with a split hoof must live upon grass and grain, or other kind of vegetation, and would not be inclined to eat flesh, dead or alive, so he considered himself perfectly safe. The possession of a perfect knowledge of your business is an absolute necessity in order to insure success.

Among the maxims of the elder Rothschild was one, all apparent paradox: "Be cautious and bold." This seems to be a contradiction in terms, but it is not, and there is great wisdom in the maxim. It is, in fact, a condensed statement of what I have already said. It is to say; "you must exercise your caution in laying your plans, but be bold in carrying them out." A man who is all caution, will never dare to take hold and be successful; and a man who is all boldness, is merely reckless, and must eventually fail. A man may go on "'change" and make fifty, or one hundred thousand dollars in speculating in stocks, at a single operation. But if he has simple boldness without caution, it is mere chance, and what he gains to-day he will lose to-morrow. You must have both the caution and the boldness, to insure success.

The Rothschilds have another maxim: "Never have anything to do with an unlucky man or place." That is to say, never have anything to do with a man or place which never succeeds, because, although a man may appear to be honest and intelligent, yet if he tries this or that thing and always fails, it is on account of some fault or infirmity that you may not be able to discover but nevertheless which must exist.

There is no such thing in the world as luck. There never was a man who could go out in the morning and find a purse full of gold in the street to-day, and another to-morrow, and so on, day after day: He may do so once in his life; but so far as mere luck is concerned, he is as liable to lose it as to find it. "Like causes produce like effects." If a man adopts the proper methods to be successful, "luck" will not prevent him. If he does not succeed, there are reasons for it, although, perhaps, he may not be able to see them.

USE THE BEST TOOLS

Men in engaging employees should be careful to get the best. Understand, you cannot have too good tools to work with, and there is no tool you should be so particular about as living tools. If you get a good one, it is better to keep him, than keep changing. He learns something every day; and you are benefited by the experience he acquires. He is worth more to you this year than last, and he is the last man to part with, provided his habits are good, and he continues faithful. If, as he gets more valuable, he demands an exorbitant increase of salary; on the supposition that you can't do without him, let him go. Whenever I have such an employee, I always discharge him; first, to convince him that his place may be supplied, and second, because he is good for nothing if he thinks he is invaluable and cannot be spared.

But I would keep him, if possible, in order to profit from the result of his experience. An important element in an employee is the brain. You can see bills up, "Hands Wanted," but "hands" are not worth a great deal without "heads." Mr. Beecher illustrates this, in this wise:

An employee offers his services by saving, "I have a pair of hands and one of my fingers thinks." "That is very good," says the employer. Another man comes along, and says "he has two fingers that think." "Ah! that is better." But a third calls in and says that "all his fingers and thumbs think." That is better still. Finally another steps in and says, "I have a brain that thinks; I think all over; I am a thinking as well as a working man!" "You are the man I want," says the delighted employer.

Those men who have brains and experience are therefore the most valuable and not to be readily parted with; it is better for them, as well as yourself, to keep them, at reasonable advances in their salaries from time to time.

DON'T GET ABOVE YOUR BUSINESS

Young men after they get through their business training, or apprenticeship, instead of pursuing their avocation and rising in their business, will often lie about doing nothing. They say; "I have learned my business, but I am not going to be a hireling; what is the object of learning my trade or profession, unless I establish myself?'"

"Have you capital to start with?"

"No, but I am going to have it."

"How are you going to get it?"

"I will tell you confidentially; I have a wealthy old aunt, and she will die pretty soon; but if she does not, I expect to find some rich old man who will lend me a few thousands to give me a start. If I only get the money to start with I will do well."

There is no greater mistake than when a young man believes he will succeed with borrowed money. Why? Because every man's experience coincides with that of Mr. Astor, who said, "it was more difficult for him to accumulate his first thousand dollars, than all the succeeding millions that made up his colossal fortune." Money is good for nothing unless you know the value of it by experience. Give a boy twenty thousand dollars and put him in business, and the chances are that he will lose every dollar of it before he is a year older. Like buying a ticket in the lottery; and drawing a prize, it is "easy come, easy go." He does not know the value of it; nothing is worth anything, unless it costs effort. Without self-denial and economy; patience and perseverance, and commencing with capital which you have not earned, you are not sure to succeed in accumulating. Young men, instead of "waiting for dead men's shoes," should be up and doing, for there is no class of persons who are so unaccommodating in regard to dying as these rich old people, and it is fortunate for the expectant heirs that it is so. Nine out of ten of the rich men of our country to-day, started out in life as poor boys, with determined wills, industry, perseverance, economy and good habits. They went on gradually, made their own money and saved it; and this is the best way to acquire a fortune. Stephen Girard started life as a poor cabin boy, and died worth nine million dollars. A.T. Stewart was a poor Irish boy; and he paid taxes on a million and a half dollars of income, per year. John Jacob Astor was a poor farmer boy, and died worth twenty millions. Cornelius Vanderbilt began life rowing a boat from Staten Island to New York; he presented our government with a steamship worth a million of dollars, and died worth fifty million. "There is no royal road to learning," says the proverb, and I may say it is equally true, "there is no royal road to wealth." But I think there is a royal road to both. The road to learning is a royal one; the road that enables the student to expand his intellect and add every day to his stock of knowledge, until, in the pleasant process of intellectual growth, he is able to solve the most profound problems, to count the stars, to analyze every atom of the globe, and to measure the firmament this is a regal highway, and it is the only road worth traveling.

So in regard to wealth. Go on in confidence, study the rules, and above all things, study human nature; for "the proper study of mankind is man," and you will find that while expanding the intellect and the muscles, your enlarged experience will enable you every day to accumulate more and more principal, which will increase itself by interest and otherwise, until you arrive at a state of independence. You will find, as a general thing, that the poor boys get rich and the rich boys get poor. For instance, a rich man at his decease, leaves a large estate to his family. His eldest sons, who have helped him earn his fortune, know by experience the value of money; and they take their inheritance and add to it. The separate portions of the young children are placed at interest, and the little fellows are patted on the head, and told a dozen times a day, "you are rich; you will never have to work, you can always have whatever you wish, for you were born with a golden spoon in your mouth." The young heir soon finds out what that means; he has the finest dresses and playthings; he is crammed with sugar candies and almost "killed with kindness," and he passes from school to school, petted and flattered. He becomes arrogant and self-conceited, abuses his teachers, and carries everything with a high hand. He knows nothing of the real value of money, having never earned any; but he knows all about the "golden spoon" business. At college, he invites his poor fellow-students to his room, where he "wines and dines" them. He is cajoled and caressed, and called a glorious good follow, because he is so lavish of his money. He gives his game suppers, drives his fast horses, invites his chums to fetes and parties, determined to have lots of "good times." He spends the night in frolics and debauchery, and leads off his companions with the familiar song, "we won't go home till morning." He gets them to join him in pulling down signs, taking gates from their hinges and throwing them into back yards and horse-ponds. If the police arrest them, he knocks them down, is taken to the lockup, and joyfully foots the bills.

"Ah! my boys," he cries, "what is the use of being rich, if you can't enjoy yourself?"

He might more truly say, "if you can't make a fool of yourself;" but he is "fast," hates slow things, and doesn't "see it." Young men loaded down with other people's money are almost sure to lose all they inherit, and they acquire all sorts of bad habits which, in the majority of cases, ruin them in health, purse and character. In this country, one generation follows another, and the poor of to-day are rich in the next generation, or the third. Their experience leads them on, and they become rich, and they leave vast riches to their young children. These children, having been reared in luxury, are inexperienced and get poor; and after long experience another generation comes on and gathers up riches again in turn. And thus "history repeats itself," and happy is he who by listening to the experience of others avoids the rocks and shoals on which so many have been wrecked.

"In England, the business makes the man." If a man in that country is a mechanic or working-man, he is not recognized as a gentleman. On the occasion of my first appearance before Queen Victoria, the Duke of Wellington asked me what sphere in life General Tom Thumb's parents were in.

"His father is a carpenter," I replied.

"Oh! I had heard he was a gentleman," was the response of His Grace.

In this Republican country, the man makes the business. No matter whether he is a blacksmith, a shoemaker, a farmer, banker or lawyer, so long as his business is legitimate, he may be a gentleman. So any "legitimate" business is a double blessing it helps the man engaged in it, and also helps others. The Farmer supports his own family, but he also benefits the merchant or mechanic who needs the products of his farm. The tailor not only makes a living by his trade, but he also benefits the farmer, the clergyman and others who cannot make their own clothing. But all these classes often may be gentlemen.

The great ambition should be to excel all others engaged in the same occupation.

The college-student who was about graduating, said to an old lawyer:

"I have not yet decided which profession I will follow. Is your profession full?"

"The basement is much crowded, but there is plenty of room up-stairs," was the witty and truthful reply.

No profession, trade, or calling, is overcrowded in the upper story. Wherever you find the most honest and intelligent merchant or banker, or the best lawyer, the best doctor, the best clergyman, the best shoemaker, carpenter, or anything else, that man is most sought for, and has always enough to do. As a nation, Americans are too superficial—they are striving to get rich quickly, and do not generally do their business as substantially and thoroughly as they should, but whoever excels all others in his own line, if his habits are good and his integrity undoubted, cannot fail to secure abundant patronage, and the wealth that naturally follows. Let your motto then always be "Excelsior," for by living up to it there is no such word as fail.

LEARN SOMETHING USEFUL

Every man should make his son or daughter learn some useful trade or profession, so that in these days of changing fortunes of being rich to-day and poor tomorrow they may have something tangible to fall back upon. This provision might save many persons from misery, who by some unexpected turn of fortune have lost all their means.

LET HOPE PREDOMINATE, BUT BE NOT TOO VISIONARY

Many persons are always kept poor, because they are too visionary. Every project looks to them like certain success, and therefore they keep changing from one business to another, always in hot water, always "under the harrow." The plan of "counting the chickens before they are hatched" is an error of ancient date, but it does not seem to improve by age.

DO NOT SCATTER YOUR POWERS

Engage in one kind of business only, and stick to it faithfully until you succeed, or until your experience shows that you should abandon it. A constant hammering on one nail will generally drive it home at last, so that it can be clinched. When a man's undivided attention is centered on one object, his mind will constantly be suggesting improvements of value, which would escape him if his brain was occupied by a dozen different subjects at once. Many a fortune has slipped through a man's fingers because he was engaged in too many occupations at a time. There is good sense in the old caution against having too many irons in the fire at once.

BE SYSTEMATIC

Men should be systematic in their business. A person who does business by rule, having a time and place for everything, doing his work promptly, will accomplish twice as much and with half the trouble of him who does it carelessly and slipshod. By introducing system into all your transactions, doing one thing at a time, always meeting appointments with punctuality, you find leisure for pastime and recreation; whereas the man who only half does one thing, and then turns to something else, and half does that, will have his business at loose ends, and will never know when his day's work is done, for it never will be done. Of course, there is a limit to all these rules. We must try to preserve the happy medium, for there is such a thing as being too systematic. There are men and women, for instance, who put away things so carefully that they can never find them again. It is too much like the "red tape" formality at Washington, and Mr. Dickens' "Circumlocution Office,"—all theory and no result.

When the "Astor House" was first started in New York city, it was undoubtedly the best hotel in the country. The proprietors had learned a good deal in Europe regarding hotels, and the landlords were proud of the rigid system which pervaded every department of their great establishment. When twelve o'clock at night had arrived, and there were a number of guests around, one of the proprietors would say, "Touch that bell, John;" and in two minutes sixty servants, with a water-bucket in each hand, would present themselves in the hall. "This," said the landlord, addressing his guests, "is our fire-bell; it will show you we are quite safe here; we do everything systematically." This was before the Croton water was introduced into the city. But they sometimes carried their system too far. On one occasion, when the hotel was thronged with guests, one of the waiters was suddenly indisposed, and although there were fifty waiters in the hotel, the landlord thought he must have his full complement, or his "system" would be interfered with. Just before dinner-time, he rushed down stairs and said, "There must be another waiter, I am one waiter short, what can I do?" He happened to see "Boots," the Irishman. "Pat," said he, "wash your hands and face; take that white apron and come into the dining-room in five minutes." Presently Pat appeared as required, and the proprietor said: "Now Pat, you must stand behind these two chairs, and wait on the gentlemen who will occupy them; did you ever act as a waiter?"

"I know all about it, sure, but I never did it."

Like the Irish pilot, on one occasion when the captain, thinking he was considerably out of his course, asked, "Are you certain you understand what you are doing?"

Pat replied, "Sure and I knows every rock in the channel."

That moment, "bang" thumped the vessel against a rock.

"Ah! be-jabers, and that is one of 'em," continued the pilot. But to return to the dining-room. "Pat," said the landlord, "here we do everything systematically. You must first give the gentlemen each a plate of soup, and when they finish that, ask them what they will have next."

Pat replied, "Ah! an' I understand parfectly the vartues of shystem."

Very soon in came the guests. The plates of soup were placed before them. One of Pat's two gentlemen ate his soup; the other did not care for it. He said: "Waiter, take this plate away and bring me some fish." Pat looked at the untasted plate of soup, and remembering the instructions of the landlord in regard to "system," replied: "Not till ye have ate yer supe!"

Of course that was carrying "system" entirely too far.

JACK DONAHUE

READ THE NEWSPAPERS

Always take a trustworthy newspaper, and thus keep thoroughly posted in regard to the transactions of the world. He who is without a newspaper is cut off from his species. In these days of telegraphs and steam, many important inventions and improvements in every branch of trade are being made, and he who don't consult the newspapers will soon find himself and his business left out in the cold.

BEWARE OF "OUTSIDE OPERATIONS"

We sometimes see men who have obtained fortunes, suddenly become poor. In many cases, this arises from intemperance, and often from gaming, and other bad habits. Frequently it occurs because a man has been engaged in "outside operations," of some sort. When he gets rich in his legitimate business, he is told of a grand speculation where he can make a score of thousands. He is constantly flattered by his friends, who tell him that he is born lucky, that everything he touches turns into gold. Now if he forgets that his economical habits, his rectitude of conduct and a personal attention to a business which he understood, caused his success in life, he will listen to the siren voices. He says:

"I will put in twenty thousand dollars. I have been lucky, and my good luck will soon bring me back sixty thousand dollars."

A few days elapse and it is discovered he must put in ten thousand dollars more: soon after he is told "it is all right," but certain matters not foreseen, require an advance of twenty thousand dollars more, which will bring him a rich harvest; but before the time comes around to realize, the bubble bursts, he loses all he is possessed of, and then he learns what he ought to have known at the first, that however successful a man may be in his own business, if he turns from that and engages ill a business which he don't understand, he is like Samson when shorn of his locks his strength has departed, and he becomes like other men.

If a man has plenty of money, he ought to invest something in everything that appears to promise success, and that will probably benefit mankind; but let the sums thus invested be moderate in amount, and never let a man foolishly jeopardize a fortune that he has earned in a legitimate way, by investing it in things in which he has had no experience.

DON'T INDORSE WITHOUT SECURITY

I hold that no man ought ever to indorse a note or become security, for any man, be it his father or brother, to a greater extent than he can afford to lose and care nothing about, without taking good security. Here is a man that is worth twenty thousand dollars; he is doing a thriving manufacturing or mercantile trade; you are retired and living on your money; he comes to you and says:

"You are aware that I am worth twenty thousand dollars, and don't owe a dollar; if I had five thousand dollars in cash, I could purchase a particular lot of goods and double my money in a couple of months; will you indorse my note for that amount?"

You reflect that he is worth twenty thousand dollars, and you incur no risk by endorsing his note; you like to accommodate him, and you lend your name without taking the precaution of getting security. Shortly after, he shows you the note with your endorsement canceled, and tells you, probably truly, "that he made the profit that he expected by the operation," you reflect that you have done a good action, and the thought makes you feel happy. By and by, the same thing occurs again and you do it again; you have already fixed the impression in your mind that it is perfectly safe to indorse his notes without security.

But the trouble is, this man is getting money too easily. He has only to take your note to the bank, get it discounted and take the cash. He gets money for the time being without effort; without inconvenience to himself. Now mark the result. He sees a chance for speculation outside of his business. A temporary investment of only $10,000 is required. It is sure to come back before a note at the bank would be due. He places a note for that amount before you. You sign it almost mechanically. Being firmly convinced that your friend is responsible and trustworthy; you indorse his notes as a "matter of course."

Unfortunately the speculation does not come to a head quite so soon as was expected, and another $10,000 note must be discounted to take up the last one when due. Before this note matures the speculation has proved an utter failure and all the money is lost. Does the loser tell his friend, the endorser, that he has lost half of his fortune? Not at all. He don't even mention that he has speculated at all. But he has got excited; the spirit of speculation has seized him; he sees others making large sums in this way (we seldom hear of the losers), and, like other speculators, he "looks for his money where he loses it." He tries again. endorsing notes has become chronic with you, and at every loss he gets your signature for whatever amount he wants. Finally you discover your friend has lost all of his property and all of yours. You are overwhelmed with astonishment and grief, and you say "it is a hard thing; my friend here has ruined me," but, you should add, "I have also ruined him." If you had said in the first place, "I will accommodate you, but

I never indorse without taking ample security," he could not have gone beyond the length of his tether, and he would never have been tempted away from his legitimate business. It is a very dangerous thing, therefore, at any time, to let people get possession of money too easily; it tempts them to hazardous speculations, if nothing more. Solomon truly said "he that hateth suretiship is sure."

So with the young man starting in business; let him understand the value of money by earning it. When he does understand its value, then grease the wheels a little in helping him to start business, but remember, men who get money with too great facility cannot usually succeed. You must get the first dollars by hard knocks, and at some sacrifice, in order to appreciate the value of those dollars.

ADVERTISE YOUR BUSINESS

We all depend, more or less, upon the public for our support. We all trade with the public—lawyers, doctors, shoemakers, artists, blacksmiths, showmen, opera stagers, railroad presidents, and college professors. Those who deal with the public must be careful that their goods are valuable; that they are genuine, and will give satisfaction. When you get an article which you know is going to please your customers, and that when they have tried it, they will feel they have got their money's worth, then let the fact be known that you have got it. Be careful to advertise it in some shape or other because it is evident that if a man has ever so good an article for sale, and nobody knows it, it will bring him no return. In a country like this, where nearly everybody reads, and where newspapers are issued and circulated in editions of five thousand to two hundred thousand, it would be very unwise if this channel was not taken advantage of to reach the public in advertising. A newspaper goes into the family, and is read by wife and children, as well as the head of the home; hence hundreds and thousands of people may read your advertisement, while you are attending to your routine business. Many, perhaps, read it while you are asleep. The whole philosophy of life is, first "sow," then "reap." That is the way the farmer does; he plants his potatoes and corn, and sows his grain, and then goes about something else, and the time comes when he reaps. But he never reaps first and sows afterwards. This principle applies to all kinds of business, and to nothing more eminently than to advertising. If a man has a genuine article, there is no way in which he can reap more advantageously than by "sowing" to the public in this way. He must, of course, have a really good article, and one which will please his customers; anything spurious will not succeed permanently because the public is wiser than many imagine. Men and women are selfish, and we all prefer purchasing where we can get the most for our money and we try to find out where we can most surely do so.

You may advertise a spurious article, and induce many people to call and buy it once, but they will denounce you as an impostor and swindler, and your business will gradually die out and leave you poor. This is right. Few people can safely depend upon chance custom. You all need to have your customers return and purchase again. A man said to me, "I have tried advertising and did not succeed; yet I have a good article."

I replied, "My friend, there may be exceptions to a general rule. But how do you advertise?"

"I put it in a weekly newspaper three times, and paid a dollar and a half for it." I replied: "Sir, advertising is like learning—'a little is a dangerous thing!'"

A French writer says that "The reader of a newspaper does not see the first mention of an ordinary advertisement; the second insertion he sees, but does not read; the third insertion he reads; the fourth insertion, he looks at the price; the fifth insertion, he speaks of it to his wife; the sixth insertion, he is ready to purchase, and the seventh insertion, he purchases." Your object in advertising is to make the public understand what you have got to sell, and if you have not the pluck to keep advertising, until you have imparted that information, all the money you have spent is lost. You are like the fellow who told the gentleman if he would give him ten cents it would save him a dollar. "How can I help you so much with so small a sum?" asked the gentleman in surprise. "I started out this morning (hiccuped the fellow) with the full determination to get drunk, and I have spent my only dollar to accomplish the object, and it has not quite done it. Ten cents worth more of whiskey would just do it, and in this manner I should save the dollar already expended."

So a man who advertises at all must keep it up until the public know who and what he is, and what his business is, or else the money invested in advertising is lost.

Some men have a peculiar genius for writing a striking advertisement, one that will arrest the attention of the reader at first sight. This fact, of course, gives the advertiser a great advantage. Sometimes a man makes himself popular by an unique sign or a curious display in his window, recently I observed a swing sign extending over the sidewalk in front of a store, on which was the inscription in plain letters,

"DON'T READ THE OTHER SIDE"

Of course I did, and so did everybody else, and I learned that the man had made all independence by first attracting the public to his business in that way and then using his customers well afterwards.

Genin, the hatter, bought the first Jenny Lind ticket at auction for two hundred and twenty-five dollars, because he knew it would be a good advertisement for him. "Who is the bidder?" said the auctioneer, as he knocked down that ticket at Castle Garden. "Genin, the hatter," was the response. Here were thousands of people from the Fifth avenue, and from distant cities in the highest stations in life. "Who is 'Genin,' the hatter?" they exclaimed. They had never heard of him before. The next morning the newspapers and telegraph had circulated the facts from Maine to Texas, and from five to ten millions off people had read that the tickets sold at auction For Jenny Lind's first concert amounted to about twenty thousand dollars, and that a single ticket was sold at two hundred and twenty-five dollars, to "Genin, the hatter." Men throughout the country involuntarily took off their hats to see if they had a "Genin" hat on their heads. At a town in Iowa it was found that in the crowd around the post office, there was one man who had a "Genin" hat, and he showed it in triumph, although it was worn out and not worth two cents. "Why," one man exclaimed, "you have a real 'Genin' hat; what a lucky fellow you are." Another man said, "Hang on to that hat, it will be a valuable heir-loom in your family." Still another man in the crowd who seemed to envy the possessor of this good fortune, said, "Come, give us all a chance; put it up at auction!" He did so, and it was sold as a keepsake for nine dollars and fifty cents! What was the consequence to Mr. Genin? He sold ten thousand extra hats per annum, the first six years. Nine-tenths of the purchasers bought of him, probably, out of curiosity, and many of them, finding that he gave them an equivalent for their money, became his regular customers. This novel advertisement first struck their attention, and then, as he made a good article, they came again.

Now I don't say that everybody should advertise as Mr. Genin did. But I say if a man has got goods for sale, and he don't advertise them in some way, the chances are that someday the sheriff will do it for him. Nor do I say that everybody must advertise in a newspaper, or indeed use "printers' ink" at all. On the contrary, although that article is indispensable in the majority of cases, yet doctors and clergymen, and sometimes lawyers and some others, can more effectually reach the public in some other manner. But it is obvious, they must be known in some way, else how could they be supported?

BE POLITE AND KIND TO YOUR CUSTOMERS

Politeness and civility are the best capital ever invested in business. Large stores, gilt signs, flaming advertisements, will all prove unavailing if you or your employees treat your patrons abruptly. The truth is, the more kind and liberal a man is, the more generous will be the patronage bestowed upon him. "Like begets like." The man who gives the greatest amount of goods of a corresponding quality for the least sum (still reserving for himself a profit) will generally succeed best in the long run. This brings us to the golden rule, "As ye would that men should do to you, do ye also to them" and they will do better by you than if you always treated them as if you wanted to get the most you could out of them for the least return. Men who drive sharp bargains with their customers, acting as if they never expected to see them again, will not be mistaken. They will never see them again as customers. People don't like to pay and get kicked also.

One of the ushers in my Museum once told me he intended to whip a man who was in the lecture-room as soon as he came out.

"What for?" I inquired.

"Because he said I was no gentleman," replied the usher.

"Never mind," I replied, "he pays for that, and you will not convince him you are a gentleman by whipping him. I cannot afford to lose a customer. If you whip him, he will never visit the Museum again, and he will induce friends to go with him to other places of amusement instead of this, and thus you see, I should be a serious loser."

"But he insulted me," muttered the usher.

"Exactly," I replied, "and if he owned the Museum, and you had paid him for the privilege of visiting it, and he had then insulted you, there might be some reason in your resenting it, but in this instance he is the man who pays, while we receive, and you must, therefore, put up with his bad manners."

My usher laughingly remarked, that this was undoubtedly the true policy; but he added that he should not object to an increase of salary if he was expected to be abused in order to promote my interest.

BE CHARITABLE

Of course men should be charitable, because it is a duty and a pleasure. But even as a matter of policy, if you possess no higher incentive, you will find that the liberal man will command patronage, while the sordid, uncharitable miser will be avoided.

Solomon says: "There is that scattereth and yet increaseth; and there is that withholdeth more than meet, but it tendeth to poverty." Of course the only true charity is that which is from the heart.

The best kind of charity is to help those who are willing to help themselves. Promiscuous almsgiving, without inquiring into the worthiness of the applicant, is bad in every sense. But to search out and quietly assist those who are struggling for themselves, is the kind that "scattereth and yet increaseth." But don't fall into the idea that some persons practice, of giving a prayer instead of a potato, and a benediction instead of bread, to the hungry. It is easier to make Christians with full stomachs than empty.

DON'T BLAB

Some men have a foolish habit of telling their business secrets. If they make money they like to tell their neighbors how it was done. Nothing is gained by this, and ofttimes much is lost. Say nothing about your profits, your hopes, your expectations, your intentions. And this should apply to letters as well as to conversation. Goethe makes Mephistophilles say: "Never write a letter nor destroy one." Business men must write letters, but they should be careful what they put in them. If you are losing money, be specially cautious and not tell of it, or you will lose your reputation.

PRESERVE YOUR INTEGRITY

It is more precious than diamonds or rubies. The old miser said to his sons: "Get money; get it honestly if you can, but get money." This advice was not only atrociously wicked, but it was the very essence of stupidity: It was as much as to say, "if you find it difficult to obtain money honestly, you can easily get it dishonestly. Get it in that way." Poor fool! Not to know that the most difficult thing in life is to make money dishonestly! Not to know that our prisons are full of men who attempted to follow this advice; not to understand that no man can be dishonest, without soon being found out, and that when his lack of principle is discovered, nearly every avenue to success is closed against him forever. The public very properly shun all whose integrity is doubted. No matter how polite and pleasant and accommodating a man may be, none of us dare to deal with him if we suspect "false weights and measures." Strict honesty, not only lies at the foundation of all success in life (financially), but in every other respect. Uncompromising integrity of character is invaluable. It secures to its possessor a peace and joy which cannot be attained without it—which no amount of money, or houses and lands can purchase. A man who is known to be strictly honest, may be ever so poor, but he has the purses of all the community at his disposal—for all know that if he promises to return what he borrows, he will never disappoint them. As a mere matter of selfishness, therefore, if a man had no higher motive for being honest, all will find that the maxim of Dr. Franklin can never fail to be true, that "honesty is the best policy."

To get rich, is not always equivalent to being successful. "There are many rich poor men," while there are many others, honest and devout men and women, who have never possessed so much money as some rich persons squander in a week, but who are nevertheless really richer and happier than any man can ever be while he is a transgressor of the higher laws of his being.

The inordinate love of money, no doubt, may be and is "the root of all evil," but money itself, when properly used, is not only a "handy thing to have in the house," but affords the gratification of blessing our race by enabling its possessor to enlarge the scope of human happiness and human influence. The desire for wealth is nearly universal, and none can say it is not laudable, provided the possessor of it accepts its responsibilities, and uses it as a friend to humanity.

The history of money-getting, which is commerce, is a history of civilization, and wherever trade has flourished most, there, too, have art and science produced the noblest fruits. In fact, as a general thing, money-getters are the benefactors of our race. To them, in a great measure, are we indebted for our institutions of learning and of art, our academies, colleges and churches. It is no argument against the desire for, or the possession of wealth, to say that there are sometimes misers who hoard money only for the sake of hoarding and who have no higher aspiration than to grasp everything which comes within their reach. As we have sometimes hypocrites in religion, and demagogues in politics, so there are occasionally misers among money-getters. These, however, are only exceptions to the general rule. But when, in this country, we find such a nuisance and stumbling block as a miser, we remember with gratitude that in America we have no laws of primogeniture, and that in the due course of nature the time will come when the hoarded dust will be scattered for the benefit of mankind. To all men and women, therefore, do I conscientiously say, make money honestly, and not otherwise, for Shakespeare has truly said, "He that wants money, means, and content, is without three good friends."

CREATING CAPITAL: MONEY-MAKING AS AN AIM IN BUSINESS
BY FREDERICK L. LIPMAN

The object of this paper is to discuss money-making; to examine its prevalence as an aim among people generally and the moral standards which obtain among those who consciously seek to make money.

The desire to make money is common to most men. Stronger or weaker, in some degree it is present in the mind of nearly every one. Now, how far does this desire grow to be an aim or object in our lives, and to what extent is such an aim a worthy one?

The typical money-maker as commonly pictured in our imagination is a narrow, grasping, selfish individual who has chosen to follow lower rather than higher ideals and who often is tempted, and always may be tempted, to employ illegitimate means for the attainment of his ends. The aims he has adopted are made to stand in opposition to the practice of certain virtues. Thus we contrast profits and patriotism; enriching one's self and philanthropy; getting all the law allows and justice; taking advantage of the other fellow and honesty; becoming engrossed in acquisition and love of family. Now, such contrasts obviously prove nothing more than that money-making is and would be a vicious aim if pursued regardless of these virtues, and it could well be replied that consideration of patriotism, philanthropy, love of family, etc., must in themselves impel one to earn and to save. "The love of money is the root of all evil" implies an exclusive devotion to acquisition that may well be criticized. But aside from this there is no doubt that amid the confused ideas held on the subject, aiming to make money is commonly regarded as in some sort of antagonism to the social virtues.

That there are other sides to the picture is recognized, however, even by the loose thought of the day. The man who earns his living, for instance, it views as one who in so far is performing a fundamental duty. Indeed, the world scorns him who cannot or will not support himself and his family. But this is only to say that one must work to-day to meet the expenditures of to-day. Is this the limit? Is it a virtue for him to work in order to spend, but a vice for him to work in order to save? What are the considerations to be observed by a man in deciding whether or not he should adopt money-making—that is, the acquisition of a surplus beyond his current needs—as one of his definite aims in life?

One consideration relates to our country. The United States is now understood to be spending about $25,000,000 per day in carrying on the war. In the last analysis this amount must be paid out of the past savings and the savings from current earnings of the people of the United States. The wealth of the nation consists mainly of the sum of the wealth of its citizens. We are therefore told to seek increased earnings and to economize in our expenditures in order to enhance the national wealth. The duty here is perfectly clear, but even if we did not have war conditions to teach us as a patriotic responsibility the necessity of earning and saving a surplus, the obligation would still be there. We owe a similar debt to our state and to our city or district. And nearer still comes the duty to one's family and to one's own future, the duty of providing for the rainy day, for old age. And it will be observed that money-making in this sense is directed to the acquisition of *net* income, it relates to that portion of one's earnings which is saved from current expenditure and becomes capital. Then we must also consider the duty to society. As we look out upon the surrounding evidences of civilization—buildings and railroads and highly cultivated fields, the machinery of production and distribution, the shops full of useful commodities—and then cast our thought backward to a time not very many years ago when all this country was a natural wilderness, we may begin to realize the magnitude of the wealth, the capital, that has come into being since then, every particle of which is due to the earnings and savings of somebody, to the surplus not consumed by the workers of the past, their unexpended and unwasted net balances year by year. Universities, churches, libraries, parks, are included in the wealth thus handed down to us. Our lives to-day may be richer and broader through this inheritance created by the industry and abstinence of our forefathers. Their business careers, now closed, we regard as the more successful in that they earned and saved a surplus, that they had a *net* income to show as the result of their work.

But these savings of the past were accumulated, after all, by comparatively few of the workers; not by the many, who lived from hand to mouth, happy-go-lucky, spending and enjoying in time of abundance, suffering in time of poverty and stress, making no provision even for their own future, still less recognizing any duty to their country or to posterity to produce economically and regulate their expenditure wisely so as to carry forward a surplus. As far as this majority is concerned we might yet be living among rocks and trees, without shelter, lacking sure supplies of food, with fig leaves to cover our nakedness. And to-day the same conditions obtain. How many persons are to be found among one's acquaintance who feel and act upon any responsibility for doing their "bit" in the creation of capital? Very few. Rather than exert himself to work with this in view, on the one hand, and to abstain from unnecessary consumption, on the other hand, the ordinary man will make to himself every excuse. He will contemn money-making as a sordid aim, readily exaggerating itself into a vice; he will dwell upon the obligations and other considerations of a higher life, this being defined as something generous and noble, a something compared with which money-making cannot be regarded as a worthy object but must be included in the class of unpleasant necessities, not to say indecencies, which ought to be relegated to the background of life; he will summon up pictures of extreme poverty, where any money received must be expended forthwith to meet urgent needs, as justifying that which in his case is the gratification of shiftless indulgence. Above all, this typical individual will not accept and act upon the idea that his affairs, his small income and expenditure, have any bearing upon the prosperity and progress of his country. The most he will keep before him is that he should pay his bills, and perhaps in some few cases, will extend the notion to the future to include provision for the bills and possible emergencies then to be met by himself and his family. Nor is this improvident attitude confined to the young, to the professional and the other non-business classes. In the business world we see it all around us; among those who "work for a living," among clerks and employees and among the so-called laboring classes it appears to be the normal attitude. People who work for salaries or wages seem characteristically to use up all their earnings in their current expenditure, to live up to their incomes without any serious attempt to save. If they pride themselves upon trying to keep out of debt, it is as much as they expect of themselves, and among them the man who attempts to go beyond this in his money affairs is certainly the exception.

One of the effects of a world-wide war is an enormously increased demand for labor at high and advancing wages, a condition that we might suppose would be greatly to the advantage of the laborer. But that will depend upon his own attitude and policy. From England, and from American towns here and there, we hear stories of the wage-earner on whom increasing income has had the effect of lessening the effort to work; who stops during the week when the higher wage scale has paid him the amount he is accustomed to regard as a week's earnings. Now, would it not seem natural to expect that any man encountering improved market conditions for his output, whether of commodity or service, would seek to turn the situation to advantage by increasing that output as largely as lay in his power? If, for instance, I can manufacture shoes to sell for $4.00 a pair and a change in market conditions is such that I can obtain $5.00 a pair, I would endeavor to produce more shoes in order to profit by the favorable market; and if thereafter the price should rise to $6.00 and $7.00 and $8.00 a pair, at each increment my efforts would be still further intensified. That, indeed, is the normal economic attitude. Fluctuations in the price level due to changes in the demand for a commodity are expected to affect, and do affect, the market supply. At a higher price, production is stimulated and more units of the commodity are brought to the market, both from new sources and from old sources. Under falling prices, on the other hand, the supply offered in the market would become automatically diminished.

This is an elementary commonplace in economics, yet the laborer to whom we have just referred does not seem to recognize it. He may find that he can earn in, say four days, an amount equal to his former earnings in six days and, therefore, at the end of the fourth day he quits work for the week. Now, obviously under such increasing wage scale, he might do one of three things:

He could quit at the end of the fourth day, having received a week's income.

He could continue working for the six days and use his surplus earnings for comforts, pleasures, and luxuries which previously he had been unable to afford.

He might work for the six days and save as much as possible of his excess earnings.

Now, what is the wise choice for the laborer? Leaving out of account special cases where he has a large family, or sickness at home, or is under some other disability which in his individual case would reduce his earning power or increase his minimum expenses, ought he not to work for the six days, putting aside all he could of the excess as savings for the future? It will be generally conceded that this is self-evident. If, viewing the narrow conditions under which the workman ordinarily lives, it should be claimed that during a period of unusual earnings self-gratification would be not only natural but measurably justifiable, the reply could be made that this is merely specious, involving assumption not in accord with the facts. Excuses of this kind we often make for ourselves in the endeavor to justify our indulgence in present pleasure rather than perform the irksome duty of self-restraint. The laborer whose ideals are such that he quits at the end of the fourth day is not the type of man who is going to spend the two holidays in pursuing higher aims in life; he is going to pass them in inaction, quite likely at the grog-shop. The man who fails to take advantage of the security for the future offered him and his family through the opportunity of saving from extraordinary earnings is one who is adding to the abnormal demand for such things as phonographs, jewelry, spirits, and tobacco. And this helps to explain the tremendous market for luxuries during wartime. Doubtless there are many workmen who follow a more rational course, who are reaping and storing the harvest for the comfort and security of themselves and their families during the winter of life. Could any one think that this policy involved an aim that was sordid, tending to draw them down, and away from higher considerations of life? Certainly a course of careful planning in one's affairs would be in so far a better course and on a higher plane than indulgence in idleness or shiftless expenditure of surplus for present luxuries, regardless of future need.

This case of the workmen under conditions of abnormal wages seems exceptional; yet the choice so presented to him is not very different fundamentally from the choice normally presented to all the rest of us.

The young man starting out in life may be as negligent of his opportunities as the workman who quits at the end of the fourth day. Or if he devotes himself properly to his vocation he may consume his earnings in current self-gratification. If, however, he will both concentrate on his work and practice self-restraint with the purpose of creating a saved surplus, all will agree in considering him as so far headed on the road towards success. In the case of the beginner this seems clear enough, but, after all, the same considerations apply to everybody else, whether in business or profession, beginners or experienced, young or old; to all of us is the same choice presented daily, and at our peril we must make it wisely. The physician, for instance, although he cannot afford to pay more attention to money-making than to the welfare of his patients, to his studies, to his professional ideals, must not, on the other hand, leave out of account these business duties and considerations which belong to him as an economic member of society. He must produce and must consume with his family, reasonably, decently and thriftily. He must aim at a surplus to store away for the future. These aims are, as a matter of course, secondary to his professional ideals, but there need be no conflict of duty. The point is that there exists a department of his activity devoted, and to be devoted, by him to his business affairs. In any event, as a man, a husband, a father, a citizen, he cannot escape from the responsibility of these business affairs. They must be conducted in some way. Shall it be well or ill? If he fails herein it may involve failure in any or all these relations—as a man, husband, father, citizen. And obviously these same considerations apply to all other men and women, whatever may be their professions, occupations, or major interests in life. Why do so many allow themselves to be dragged along, living from hand-to-mouth, in fear of the knock of the bill collector at the door? Why do we associate money questions with that which is unhappy, unfortunate, down-at-the-heel, with fear and misery? Barring mere accidents, it is because we are careless, shiftless; because we do not face the problem manfully, practice reasonable self-restraint, consider the subject in its complexity and decide upon, and carry out, a constructive programme. Even if one happens to possess wealth, he is not exempt. Indeed, large wealth involves still greater necessity for care in the conduct of one's pecuniary affairs. The rich man is said to have perplexities and responsibilities which are unknown to those in moderate circumstances. In fine, everyone must face these money questions or be driven by them.

Those who live on fixed incomes, whether from salary or investment, may find it impossible to make any direct attempt to make money; for them the problem is to be confronted and mastered on its other side, the side of spending and saving, that the income may be apportioned as wisely as possible for the purposes of living. But during the last few years a new factor has entered into the money problems of the individual, often adding to his trials, often adding to his self-made excuses, and especially burdensome to the man on fixed income. We refer to the high cost of living. Here it is, however, that the wage earner can do something in self-protection, for the level of prices may be in some measure affected by his policy in handling his earnings.

A period of high wages is accompanied by and is in some sense an incident of a high level of prices. Now we recognize high wages, considered in itself, as beneficial to the community, for it gives opportunity, at least, for comforts in life and a provision for the future that otherwise would be lacking. But if prices have advanced as much as wages, the apparent improvement to the laborer is merely in nominal wages, while that which alone can benefit him is higher real wages. Now let us see what the workman could do to advance real wages as contrasted with nominal wages.

What will be the effect on prices of the use of surplus earnings during a period of high wages?

If the surplus earnings are expended, they will be used either in meeting the higher prices of customary commodities, or in meeting these advanced prices and also in purchasing additional commodities. The first case will occur only if, and when, the advance in price equals the advance in wages, for only in that event will the new wages just cover the new cost of customary commodities. Then this expenditure of the entire income in customary commodities tends to keep up the price level and any benefit from higher wages disappears.

In the second case, so far as the worker spends his surplus earnings in meeting advanced prices for customary commodities, he tends to maintain prices at the higher level, and so far as he buys additional commodities, he increases the demand for them and tends further to advance the price level.

If, on the other hand, the worker will save from his surplus earnings, he will increase the community's capital, and this will tend, directly or indirectly, to cause the production of further commodities, so increasing the supply of commodities and therefore tending to reduce prices.

In any case, the worker should save as much as possible, as this tends to reduce the price level and so to better his condition. Or, putting it more simply, in time of high wages the worker ought to produce as much as possible and consume as little as possible, both influences tending to increase the stock of commodities for his ultimate gain and for that of the community.

In fact, a high level of prices may be due measurably to some wasting of the world's capital—as in war, for instance—and then the only antidote is to restore the capital, a movement that would doubtless occur anyway in time but which could be greatly accelerated through a general adoption of habits of thrift and saving throughout a community.

This then, though small, is something definite that we can contribute to the material advancement of mankind and, like the duty in this connection to our nation, to our families and ourselves, it consists in creating capital; that is, earning as much as we can and, in any event, even if our earnings are fixed, managing the income thriftily, and carrying forward as large a net result as possible.

We turn now from the mass of mankind, on the whole so singularly neglectful of these responsibilities, to the few in number who constitute the creators of capital, to whom are due so much of the comforts, the conveniences, and the material advantages that go to make civilized life possible. Now these few are found in every rank in life. They may be rich or poor, professional or business men, employer or employee, old or young, male or female. The characteristic is their habit of thrift, of definitely adopting money-making as an aim, of spending less than they earn. It is astonishing what a small percentage of mankind they are. The Income Tax returns in the United States for 1916 showed that out of a population of 104,000,000 people those with taxable incomes aggregated only 336,652, about one in three hundred. But whatever be the rank of the individual practicing this thrift he is headed in the right direction and he tends to reach the point of relative competence, of independence in his pecuniary affairs.

Preëminent in the class of the thrifty we think of the man of affairs; the business enterprise indeed is supposed to be the money-maker, *par excellence*. Money-making is in fact considered as its *raison d'être*; it is as a money-maker that the business man is contemned by some and envied by many.

Now money-making and money values occupy a special place in business enterprise, due to the fact that on economic principles such money value becomes the best test—perhaps the only true test—of the workableness and success of business efforts. In the complicated activities of the world's work, where each man, each undertaking, each business unit, respectively, is striving primarily for its own advantage, how is it, among all this pulling and pushing, this competition, that the social income is distributed so nearly in accordance with the individual contribution? Even if we admit that many persons fail to get a fair share, that there is gross inequality here and there, still after all, a student of mankind's activities in production, distribution, and consumption must marvel at the extent to which the rewards approximate the value of contribution. Now this is made possible by money considered as a measure of relative values, by the standard or test of fitness embodied in the thought, Will it pay, and to what extent will it pay? If I have in mind some new invention that will perhaps confer benefits on mankind, the best test of its practicability and utility will be, Will it pay, will people buy it, pay money for it? If an improvement in process is proposed, the question is, Will it pay? If the young man starts out in life with high ideals and a reasonably good opinion of his own abilities, an opinion fostered perhaps by fond parents and admiring friends, the question is, Will these abilities fit in with the world's needs? Will they supply a real demand, will they be serviceable? The best means of ascertaining this, although it may be only a rough estimate and although errors occasionally creep in is, will they pay? Can he sell these services for real money? This criterion is practically omnipresent in the world of affairs. It is based on economic necessity, and although here and there it may be charged with cruelties, with serious blunders, it is, on the whole, a remarkably accurate standard. We see this more clearly where we attempt to substitute some other criterion for ranking the soldiers in the battle of life. We can note, for instance, the inferior type and character, generally speaking, of men elected to office by the suffrages of their fellow citizens, compared with men who reach positions of authority in business and other enterprises through the pressure of these economic principles. Again, consider the nation that has attempted to improve on economic distribution of power by evolving a government which places the power in the hands of those best fitted to govern, a ruling class which aims directly at efficiency, a select class but necessarily self-selected, thus supplanting an economic régime by a military régime—successful truly in certain forms of economic efficiency through a more rigid and compact organization, but destructive of the initiative, the evolutionary growth, the fundamental development, the liberties of the people. Contrast this with the freedom, happiness, and progress of a nation of shop-keepers. Now this economic régime, with its individual instances of cruelty, like the cruelties of nature, does on the whole tend to develop men, to require their best efforts, to make them come forward and upward. Thus, in this interplay of economic forces, wealth, or money, or profits stands out as a primary object of attainment, and becomes the incentive to the complex efforts which tend to benefit the individual, the community, and the nation.

The business enterprise then directs its attention to profits, because, from mere economic necessity, profits are the criterion of the true success of the enterprise, that is, its serviceability to mankind. Here we distinguish between the shortsighted man, who aims at immediate returns, and the farsighted man, whose eye is fixed on the future, who verily desires the profits, but desires them in the long run. But this is only a manifestation of human nature as we find it in every field. We always note a deficiency in the man whose life is lived for the present, for immediate enjoyment: in him we see the typical pleasure-seeker, peculiarly prone to temptation, to break the rules of life, to indulge himself at the expense of others or of his own future. He is characteristically the weakling, the wrongdoer. And we contrast him with the man of character, who stands superior to an immediate environment, who will not disregard the distant future, the absent neighbor, the invisible God. And so in the economic world it is the whole life period which is to be regarded when aims are chosen. Profits as a goal for the long run do not antagonize moral principles. "Honesty is the best policy" and "Do unto others as you would have others do unto you" are maxims of good business; and that economic principles do not conflict with them is shown by the fact that they tend towards profits in the long run. This is not to assert that mankind in business is perfect. In every period of economic advance into a new environment, men try new experiments, as during the development of the great modern corporation in the period following the Civil War in this country and, earlier than that, in the era of railroad building. They have tried new experiments in ethics as they have in physics, in chemistry, in economics. They have attempted to replace honesty by camouflage, the golden rule by self-aggrandizement. But these attempts are not successful and so they become discredited; they do not work because inherently they cannot last, and inability to endure is fatal to the purposes of any economic undertaking. We are emphasizing the fact that business is necessarily conducted for the long run, the very nature of success implying permanence. A man may take some criminal advantage of an opportunity: he may abscond with money entrusted to him; he may abuse the confidence reposed in him by an employer, by a customer; he may obtain an immediate profit by misrepresentation. But no one could expect such things to last; he could not possibly be building an enduring structure; such a course could not in the end promise him profits, or any other kind of success. A properly conducted business enterprise then is concerned with making profits in the long run; that is to say, in accordance with accepted notions of business conduct; in short, according to rules of the game, and this involves conformity with a standard, a standard of giving good value for what one gets.

We must next distinguish between gross profits and net profits. The merchant or manufacturer naturally desires to do a large business, he points with pride to the increase in his sales this year over last year. The larger his turnover the smaller the proportionate amount of his overhead expenses that must be borne per unit of product, and other economies follow large-scale production or distribution. He may occasionally be desirous of increasing his output even when it entails a disproportionate increase in his expenditures, with the idea that he can later occupy himself with reducing these expenses and in the meanwhile the goodwill of his enterprise will have gained from the larger circle of customers. Such is the case with a new enterprise that often starts out with the expectation of little or no profits during its early years, when it is gathering a clientèle and learning to distribute its product with economy. All these, however, are special cases. The normal situation is that the business enterprise is aiming at net profits, having an interest in large sales, heavy transactions and gross profits only so far as these are expected to lead finally to net profits, the real goal. Now these net profits are, of course, the remainder of earnings left on hand after providing for all costs and expenses, for depreciation and every other factor causing loss, destruction, and deterioration during the business period under consideration. In short, the business capital as it was at the beginning of the period is first fully restored and made intact at the end of the period before a net profit emerges. This net profit therefore becomes in a true sense a creation of new capital and may indeed be retained in the business as an addition to capital funds. Even when it is paid out in dividends, partly or wholly, it becomes new capital in the hands of the individual stockholders who then in their private capacity may of course spend it, but by proper investment may keep it permanently stored as capital. It is the creation of capital then, that is in reality the ultimate money-making aim of the business enterprise.

We can now summarize the attitude and policy of the typical business man in his money-making aim as follows:

In seeking profits he is actuated by economic necessity.

His goal is profits in the long run, which involves conformity with economic and ethical standards, and net profits, which implies the creation of capital.

The creation of capital we cannot fail to recognize as a worthy aim. It has given mankind much of all that mankind possesses and constitutes the foundation upon which civilization largely rests. The advancement in the arts and sciences has been in no small degree stimulated by the demands of business enterprise for new methods of creating capital and we may believe that should the time arrive when this motive should fail, when men should grow to be indifferent in their attitude towards profits, the ensuing stagnation would affect every department of human endeavor. Of this we may be assured even when we remember that money-making, and what goes with it, is not the only aim in life.

After cataloguing so much that is virtuous in the pursuit of money-making the suggestion is inevitable that there must be some other side to it, that the common views of the rapacity of the money-maker cannot be wholly unfounded. What then are the vices of the money-making aim? In examining this question we shall first brush aside some things to which we have already referred. The pathological cases of mere crime, of sharp practice, of taking advantage of others, while mounting up into distressingly high figures considered absolutely, are much less important relatively; that is, they are infrequent and scarce enough to avoid obscuring the rule which they violate, the rule that honesty is indispensable in economics as well as in ethics. What we must now investigate is any vicious tendencies that may be found in the money-making aim when followed normally and according to its own accepted principles. Of such degenerative tendencies we seem to find two: first, the tendency to that excess which becomes a vice; and second, the tendency to a disregard of other considerations in life through too exclusive a devotion to acquisitiveness. But upon further thought we must see that these two tendencies flow together and become one, for too much devotion to money-getting and too little attention to the other purposes of life are, after all, expressions of the same thing. Perhaps a man may err in excessive devotion to any object of life but we must admit that in the pursuit of gain the evil tendency to exaggerated absorption in the one aim is promoted through a cooperation with his natural selfishness. Of all the fields of human endeavor, here is one that peculiarly fits in with self-seeking, with disregard for others, which may drag a man downward, making him small and mean, unhappy and uncharitable, while apparently attaining the goal at which he has aimed. Not every man, while concentrating upon money-making, is consciously seeking his country's welfare, the amelioration of life for the many, the uplift of posterity, even if he rigidly adheres to the accepted rules of the game, to the code of business honor. This brings us back to the popular picture of the money-maker, grasping, sordid, narrow-minded. There are such people. I believe them to be rare, but whether there are many of them to-day or not, it is a type tending to disappear in the environment of modern business which offers its inducements and rewards to him who does, who becomes, who renders service, not to the sordid seeker for gain. Barring an occasional exception, such an exclusive aim is not that of the man of large affairs, the business leader, the conspicuously successful man. It is not Harriman, nor Edison, nor Weinstock, nor Marshall Field, nor Peabody, nor is it the heads of our big corporations of to-day. Such men are money-makers, creators of capital, builders of large enterprise, but their aim at profits while genuine is only incidental to their main purpose of doing, of becoming better able to achieve, of rendering service. When the beginner in business approaches an experienced friend for advice, he is told to work as hard and as faithfully as possible, to study his business, to seek to improve himself—in other words, to concentrate his whole strength on the giving of service, for his wages or salary will take care of itself. The experienced man knows well that this holds just as truly for all ranks in the business world and that the higher one ascends in responsibilities, the more he must give and do; indeed the leading positions in the business world are occupied by men who produce tremendously, whose value to themselves and others lies in what they accomplish, and this—not what they get—is the criterion of success among men of experience, among those in charge of enterprises, who are on the lookout for leaders of this type.

Here we have the remedy for the tendency backed by natural selfishness towards undue devotion to gain: such narrowness simply does not work, it is crowded out by competition with the superior efficiency of broader motives. And while, here and there, the type continues to exist, its development in new cases is discouraged by every instance illustrating the relative success—in all senses—attained by those who make it their chief aim to produce, to render service. Just as the physician bestows his first thought upon his patient, these superior business men give first consideration to their profession, for so they regard it, and this tends to assure their success, just as it does that of the physician, and to become the standardized ideal for lesser men.

It is indeed clearly self-evident that on many accounts the man in business must give attention primarily to the service he is trying to render. The clerk in the store must devote himself mainly to his customers, to his merchandise, to his other duties, not to his salary. And so with the department manager, and so with the general manager, whether of a store, a railroad company, or other activity; the immediate daily problem for all lies in the rendering of a service, the producing of a commodity, or the doing of the thing for which the business enterprise exists. This concentration upon output is furthermore required by competition which whips the producer into line and often makes it a matter of business life and death that one should make progress in method and quality. That his shoes wear is a matter of pride to the shoe manufacturer. "Blank tires are good tires" is not to be regarded as merely a boastful advertisement. If it was it would not pay the advertising cost.

Money-making as an aim thus becomes subsidiary to the characteristic activities of the enterprise, it is in a sense a by-product. But the money-making aim is there, although perhaps in the background. It is furnishing the power under which the enterprise operates. More than that, it is the gauge indicating the prosperity or lack of prosperity of the enterprise, its progress, its fitting in with the needs of life. In short, the money-making aim spurs on the business enterprise, just as the weekly or monthly pay spurs on the humble worker; but in each case the main attention is given, and necessarily given, to the work to be performed.

Let us now consider some of the implications of this concentration on rendering service. The directed effort of each man to the production of the utility characteristic of his business, tends to result in his learning to conduct that specific activity with a high degree of skill, and with an increasingly valuable fund of experience. So highly specialized does he become that it will be quite impossible for anyone hitherto a stranger in that sphere to conduct it as well. Therefore in an age of coordinated effort the more a man has of accumulated knowledge and facility in handling a certain kind of affair and the better fitted, therefore, he is to continue and to progress along that line, the less relatively he is able to undertake the affairs of some other kind with which he is not familiar. We commonly feel free to criticize a railroad, a newspaper, a large business house, perhaps a university, with which we may have casual contact, but the fact is there are few competent critics outside of the ranks of the enterprise itself or of those carrying on activities that are directly similar. In a word, through this focusing of attention, a man will come to be exhaustively familiar with his own occupation, while possessing a merely superficial acquaintance with the theories, customs, and responsibilities of those of others. The wise man therefore argues the necessity of confining himself to the field in which he has become expert and will avoid taking chances in some outside direction wherein he is not familiar. One of the most common and disheartening experiences in the money-making and money-saving of the thrifty is that after having both worked hard and practiced self-restraint, the resultant savings are often put into some enterprise that turns out badly, and the whole effort is thus thrown away. Generally this happens because he has violated the rule we have just stated; he has ventured his savings in unfamiliar fields, ignorantly he has rushed in where the better informed would have feared to tread. Such so-called investments are in reality highly speculative. They involve risks which are unknown and altogether to be avoided. Now no one speculates in his own legitimate business, for there he is acquainted with the hazards which, he has learned, require the best of knowledge and the greatest of prudence. It is the allurement of the unknown that tempts him to seek unearned profits through speculation in outside regions where, in the nature of the case, the chances must be against him. Now speculation has its proper place in business: there are certain inherent hazards that must be undertaken, mainly to be found in the risk of the seasons in the production of crops, and the risk of the future in undeveloped enterprise. These risks must be carried by somebody, but clearly they constitute an activity for specialists who study conditions, becoming relatively expert in determining how and when to act. These specialists are drawn principally from two classes: First, the professional speculator, who knows his markets and makes a business of buying and selling future risks; such men perform a great service in handling our seasonal crops and in other directions, and are entitled to a reasonable profit. Second, the man of wealth who may use part of his surplus in the risks of undeveloped enterprise; although it is probable that in the end his losses and expenses will outweigh his gains, he can afford to take chances of such experiments in the hope that success will follow in some of them; furthermore, he can regard the outlay as a contribution to the advancement of mankind. For the rest of us, however, outside of these two classes, it is our business to keep away from speculation whether in oil wells, flying machines, in new factories, or in real estate: in the long run, we cannot get something for nothing and money-making efforts that are ethically valid thus coincide with those that are selfishly desirable, namely, the efforts to obtain the payment, the profit, that arises from a valuable service performed or commodity produced. Too often men who follow this rule in their regular occupation depart from it in the use of their saved surplus funds. They feel that their savings ought to make them money, as they say.

Now savings can be employed in one of three ways: They may be used as capital by the owner; or they may be put out in investments—that is, used or utilized as capital in the business of another; or, third, they may be wasted in gambling or speculation. As a matter of course, the employment as additional capital in one's own enterprise is generally the most desirable wherever applicable, but this is a use of limited scope, relating to but few of the people engaged in productive activity who earn and save a surplus. The main resource for such accumulations is in safe investments, in the bonds and securities of our own country and those of well established enterprises. Not many among our embryo capitalists possess the experience or skill requisite for the safe and proper investment of their funds, they must rely upon the advice of others. But whom can they trust? The demand for investment advice has not failed to call forth a supply of advisers, and elaborate are the schemes designed to lure the unwary. But, generally speaking, the man who falls into the clutches of these birds of prey has himself to blame, for the reason that the temptations they offer are appeals to the illegitimate desire to get something for nothing or to the foolish notion that one can get-rich-quick in some way whispered about by a stranger, and out of sheer benevolence. The fact is that the wise man will dismiss all thought of making money out of his investments; he will seek only the moderate return which alone is consistent with safety; and with this policy, will turn a deaf ear to any so-called opportunity which promises big profits. We can summarize the matter by saying that concentration upon one's business and service implies that one should not attempt to make money elsewhere.

This concentration on one's affairs therefore grows into a sort of practical system in which each member of the business community is looking after some function or activity to the exclusion of other things. And so the world's work is carried on to the best advantage, each function being filled by those particular men who have become relatively expert therein. From this system arises a business habit or method not always understood by the young and inexperienced, by the non-business person. We refer to the practice in trade of leaving to each individual, to each enterprise, to each organization, the responsibility for looking out for its own interests when having dealings with others. *Caveat emptor*—let the buyer beware—expresses an extreme development of this, and in its common signification, that each side is to be permitted and expected to take any advantage of the other side that it may be able to secure, it describes a state of warfare rather than of business. In buying and selling, in aiming to obtain the most favorable terms for each line of his activity, in meeting conditions of competition, in all these relations, the business man is endeavoring to better himself and may doubtless be tempted here and there to forget the interests of the other party to the transaction. But to yield to such temptation would merely be to abuse a principle which on the whole is sanctioned by the requirements of economic efficiency. This principle is that the nearest approximation to effective justice in business transactions is reached when on each side the parties devote themselves to their respective interests and points of view. If A has a house for sale and B is a prospective buyer, the essence of the possible transaction between the two is that A's idea of the value of the property is different from B's idea of that value; or at any rate that A sees less value in it to him than does B to B. This is of course typical of all business transactions—the seller desires the money above the commodity, the buyer prefers the commodity to the money. The seller and the buyer each dwells naturally upon his own idea of value. This is altogether desirable, not to say indispensable, and is characteristic of every relation of business, wherever two men buy and sell, employ one another, or have other dealings together. The situation is somewhat the same as in a law suit where the duty of the attorney for the plaintiff is to make every point that fairly can be made for the plaintiff, while the attorney on the other side must correspondingly make every point that can properly be made for the defendant. Each side is supposed to look after the interest of that side. Similarly, in a business organization, say a railroad, when some new project is under consideration it will be submitted to the engineer, to the chemist, to the attorney, to the practical transportation man, and in each of these departments it is expected that the wisdom born of experience in the particular function will be brought to bear. The engineer speaks with authority on engineering questions, the lawyer on legal questions, the transportation man on the practical working out of the project; and, normally, the criticisms and contribution of each are confined to his own function. In short, the régime of economic self-interest results in leaving to each the responsibility which he is most competent to assume, that in which he is most expert, which thereby receives the best attention that generally speaking it could have. Nor are correctives lacking for the abuses which may enter in through an overdevelopment of self-interest. *Caveat emptor* becomes discredited as an unmodified basis of human action. The golden rule is increasingly seen to constitute a foundation demanded by economics as well as by ethics. The trend to-day is away from indifference to the interests of those with whom we deal. The successful merchant will not attempt to make a profit through sales which he knows would not benefit the purchaser, for that would not measure up to the test, Will it pay? The value of a business depends largely on its goodwill and too much money and effort are spent in advertising and other means of building up a clientèle to make men conceive it to be to their interest to deal sharply with their customers.

In the efforts of scientists to seek out and establish new methods, new principles, the success of an experiment is to be determined, I suppose, by the test, Will it work? Does it yield effective results? Similarly, in economics, the science of mankind in its production, distribution and consumption of material things, the test of utility and efficiency is, Will it pay? that being the standard of workableness in the application of that science.

We have attempted, therefore, in this analysis of money-making to apply this test, because the practice or habit or influence that pays is that which is in accord so far with the principles underlying this branch of social science. We have seen, according to this standard, that it is the duty of all to adopt money-making as a conscious aim; that the money is to be economically used, the final object being net profit, that balance or remainder which is carried forward as created capital. Inability to increase a fixed income does not absolve one from the duty of doing one's part in the creation of capital through thrift and saving. The business enterprise, moreover, is required by economic necessity to aim at money-making—meaning, however, profits in the long run rather than immediate or temporary gains. Such permanent returns can only be sought through adherence to ethical principles and although this aim at profits becomes the power plant which drives the business machine, the latter gives its energies and attention more directly to the rendering of service.

Concentration upon service tends to make a man relatively efficient therein, but argues a relative unfamiliarity with the field of others, from which we infer the advisability of confining one's activity to the thing he has learned to do best. As an example of this, he should avoid placing his surplus capital or savings in outside enterprises where they will partake of risks that are unknown to him, nor should he attempt to employ his savings at all with the purpose of making money, unless, indeed, he can use them as capital in his own business. The focusing of attention on one's own function also implies and explains the custom of placing upon participants in a business transaction the responsibility each for his own side, a custom which is economically justified but which must be kept within proper limits, as is fully recognized by the business men who are successful and who therefore become models or examples for the guidance of other men, influencing the latter towards high ideals.

We have found, on the other hand, that apart from men in charge of business enterprise, the burden of providing thus for man's welfare and development is assumed by very few, the vast majority, whether in professional or business employment, treating it with neglect and contempt. They think, perhaps, that they are aiming at higher things, or that their efforts would not sufficiently count, or they do not give the matter any sturdy thought; while the underlying motive, often unconscious, is simply an unwillingness to practice self-restraint. It is self-indulgence, we must conclude, that is to be overcome if we are to meet this responsibility in a manly way, visualizing it with sufficient clearness to see that thrift, the creation of capital for one's self and for the race, comes into no necessary conflict with any other proper aim in life, but on the contrary constitutes a fundamental duty to society, to the state, to one's family, to his own future, to his self-respect.

THE CONFLICT BETWEEN PRIVATE MONOPOLY AND GOOD CITIZENSHIP
BY JOHN GRAHAM BROOKS

For a special purpose, I have had occasion to examine with care the comments upon American life and institutions made by foreign critics during the period that extends from the later part of the eighteenth century up to the present time. If one puts aside the frivolous and ill-tempered studies and considers alone the fairer and more competent observers, the least pleasant of all the criticisms is that we are essentially a lawless people.

If the critic, like de Tocqueville and Miss Martineau, had sympathy and admiration for us, the revealed lawlessness came as an astonishment, because it seemed to upset all sorts of pretty theories about democracy. The doctrinaires had worked out to perfection the idea that a people who could freely make and unmake their own laws would, for that plain reason, respect the laws. Of course, a people who had laws thrust upon them from above would hate them and disobey them. But a democracy would escape this temptation.

It was apparently an amusement of many of these writers to collect, as did the jaunty author of "Peter Simple" in his Diary, interminable pages from our own press to illustrate the general contempt for those laws which really interfered with pleasures or economic interests. Harriet Martineau drove through Boston on the day when Garrison was being dragged through the streets. The flame of her indignation burned high; but it burned with new heat when she found that the very best of Boston culture and respectability would not lift a finger or pay a copper to have the law enforced in Mr. Garrison's favor. Beacon Street and Harvard professors told her that the victim was a disreputable agitator, richly deserving what he got. They seemed to think this English lady very cranky and unreasonable. The mob had the entire sympathy of the best people in the community, and that should satisfy her. De Tocqueville had an awakening at a polling-booth in Pennsylvania that in the same way disturbed all his presuppositions about us.

It is not my purpose to bristle up and strike back at these critics of American behavior. Amid possible exaggeration, they are telling a great deal of truth about us. It is a truth that it has its own natural history. A long adventurous border-life was in some respects the great fact of the nineteenth century in moulding our national habits. A large part of the population lived under conditions where no appeal to legal restraints was possible. There were no courts,--no police. The whole constructive work of life was thrown so absolutely upon the man fighting his life-battle alone, that excessive individualistic habits were formed. Every self-reliant instinct was developed until it became a law unto itself. They do not, says de Tocqueville of the Americans, ask help. They do not "appeal." They understand that everything rests with themselves. Every immigrant of those days had come from what Freeman calls "overgoverned" countries. They escaped from highly organized social constraints to have their fling on a continent as illimitable in extent as it was in the prizes which its natural resources offered. That such a large proportion of the strong lived this free border-life through the entire century has resulted in making a standard of individualistic action almost dominant in the community.

There is, first, this natural history of extreme individualistic habits and of their reactions on our whole national life. There is, further, the almost universal concentration on wealth-production as a means of winning what average men most crave in this world. What the strong of any race work for is not, ultimately, money, it is social power. This power has many symbols in a monarchy. There are titles and decorations for which armies of able men will do hard public service for years. This same passion is as lively in the United States as in Germany, but we exclude the symbols. Wealth everywhere gives power, but with us it is almost the only symbol that has wide and practical recognition. This passion, working in a vigorous people upon the resources which the United States offers, has intensified the competitive struggle in industry to a degree hitherto unknown in the world. This struggle has absorbed the thought and strength of the people to an extent without known parallel.

It is the magnitude and stress of this competition that have bent and subdued politics to business ends. The engendered business rivalries in this game develop qualities that are indifferent to laws.

The last ten years of investigation have disclosed one further reason for heedlessness of law. The chances of promotion among the abler and more ambitious young men in the service of large concerns are known to depend on the fact of a good showing in their departments. Can they keep down expenses? Can they enlarge and maintain sales? These have been the supreme tests for rapid and sure promotion. When these are done, few questions are asked by manager or director. Among the largest interests in this country, and among all interests that have to do with franchises and legislation, skill to evade laws may have the highest value in a fight against competitors. A magnate recently accused of law-breaking denies it roundly, and it may be with honesty. When the evidence of long-practiced frauds against the laws in his own business is produced, he insists that he never knew it. But he also turns on the light: "I do not ask my heads of departments _how_ they succeed; it is enough for me that they do succeed." This explains, but does not excuse, the guilt.

I make no use here of theory. I am thinking of definite large business interests in which the evil will remain as common as it is inevitable so long as the business is unregulated and its shady practices concealed from public authorities and public opinion. In some of our huge concerns it is the traditional procedure to bring the various heads of departments together at regular intervals and pit them against each other as if running a race for life. What is the showing that each can make against the other? Has this one cut down the cost of his product; has he reduced this or that item of expenditure; has he got the most out of the workmen under his charge; has he been able to dodge practical difficulties--legal, sanitary, or any other--that stood in his way?

In this relentless contest before their superiors, the foreman or agent learns that the one key to favor and advancement is that no other shall make a better showing. If he can safely get this superior result out of his labor group, that is one way; if he can reach his end by introducing children under age, or by any other questionable device, the temptation is there in the subtlest form it can assume for the average man. When, recently, a swarm of sharp practices came out in another of the great concerns whose products reach half the homes of the nation, the man at the top doubtless told the truth when he replied: "In my position, it is not my business to know those details. I have no time except for the results sent in." Thus the president or director stands apart from and above this underworld of tolerated illegalities.

Here, then, are three reasons for lack of obedience to the law,--the long border struggle, the excessive concentration upon wealth-exploitation, and the ways through which successful subordinates are rewarded in severely competitive industries.

But another, weightier reason must now be added,--namely, our private monopolies with their influence and reactions on our whole community life. In the earlier and looser stages of development, when vast resources still remain unappropriated, private monopoly may aid a city or a nation. At first no public protection of fish and game is necessary, but the pressure of population will eventually compel a common rule to which the individual must submit. As surely as a growing town sooner or later requires a common water-supply, a common drainage, common sanitary provisions, and regulated hack charges, just so surely will the private monopoly somewhere and at some time require strict social control,--that is, control from the point of view of all of us and not from that of a few money-makers. A generation ago the stripping of our forests did not matter vitally. The interests that were to suffer from this stripping had not appeared. To-day a forestry policy derived absolutely from the common, social point of view has become a necessity so commanding that the nation's attention is at last caught. A generation ago no one had even guessed at the franchise-value of our streets,--not even those of New York city. After Jacob Sharp had made these values known, a struggle began which reads like an Arabian tale. It is a story of business and political corruption that has gone on in varying degrees in scores of our cities and in scores of great industries where strong men have been fighting to get control of mines, forests, lands, and oil, the development of which depended on favorable transportation. The carrying trade--whether of goods or people--is never to be omitted in this story. Until very recent years, this mother of monopolies, the railroad, was thought of as a purely private possession.

A dozen years ago one of our ablest railroad lawyers (often before the United States Supreme Court with great cases) told me it had long been one of his intellectual amusements to try to force into the heads of railroad presidents the fact that their ownership of that kind of property was profoundly different from the ownership of a horse or a grocery store. "I finally," he said, "had to give it up." It meant nothing to them that society had given them stupendous privileges which qualified their ownership. These franchise-grants once in their pockets, everything that was built upon them came to be used in any conceivable game to enrich the owner.

Properly informed persons no longer discuss whether it is right and moral to allow railroad magnates to do as they like--to act as if these properties were strictly a private possession. We know, at last, how society has suffered from leaving this form of ownership so long without social control. We have seen the devastating conflict between unregulated possession of this kind of property and all the higher welfare of the community. If we add to the railway the common city monopolies of lighting and transportation; if we add industries in iron and steel, much of our mining, oil, and forest exploitation, all of which, in connection with railways, take on inevitably the form of monopoly, we have the whole buccaneer-group that has done upon our politics the deadly work, which we know so well that its retelling is a thing to avoid from very weariness.

Though a dozen other cities would serve as well, look for a moment at the monopoly of the New York street-railways. A people, careless and ignorant of their own interests, so far give away the rights in their streets, that a few men get them into their possession. With the grip once fast upon this power, it becomes not a machinery primarily to serve the people: primarily it becomes an enginery to filch vast unearned increments from the public. It becomes a device for gambling, with the dice so heavily loaded in your favor that you cannot lose. You change power from one kind to another; you merge one line with another or with the whole; you create holding companies; and at every change you recapitalize. Your million dollars is turned into five or ten or twenty millions, in order that multiplied dividends taken from the public may drop into private pockets. Every bit of bookkeeping meant for the public eye is a mass of jugglery. If you are frightened by the challenge of an indignant public, the most important records are destroyed. Surplus funds belonging to the stockholders are freely loaned to personal friends or put to private speculative ventures.

This shell-game has gone on decade after decade, so gayly that it seems as if it were a delight to the American people to have their pockets picked. And yet, let us say it over and over again, the pocket-picking is not the worst of it. That the people's money should be used to debauch their own chosen representatives in city and state legislatures is the uttermost evil. Part and parcel of the uttermost evil is the resulting suspicion and distrust that eat their way deep through the masses of the wage-earning world. Not to mention their own trade papers, or the socialistic sheets with the scandals of high and low finance, wage-earners have only to read the capitalistic sheets, presidential messages, and summarized reports from scores of legislative committees, in order to believe that almost everything investigated--insurance, city traction companies, mining syndicates, railway finance--is heavy with rottenness. Anyone interested enough to run through the files of the distinctively labor press at the present moment, will find a body of convinced opinion about those who control us industrially that has an extremely ugly look. The labor-world is drawing the only natural inference it can from the data given.

How often we have seen within a year or two the lament that the efficiency of labor has lessened in many of our great industries! What in Heaven's name can we expect? If that labor-world believes what is everywhere cried on the housetops about the crooked exploiting devices of these monopolies, why should not its interest and its fidelity fall off? The law of cause and effect will work here as it works elsewhere in the universe. Labor is learning that unfair industrial privilege flouts every essential principle of democratic government. The real iniquity of it is hidden from us until we see that secrecy, cunning, and unscrupulousness may be good pecuniary assets. Yes, this has to be plainly stated. A man who should happen to have the people's interest really at heart could not be an active partner in the worst of these monopolies. The unscrupulous, the men bent upon the stock-watering game and their own immediate enrichment, would crowd the honest men to the wall. Every line of least resistance is with the get-rich-quick type of manager. To hold his power and to corrupt us politically; to appropriate continuous unearned increment through overcapitalization, he must work not for the public good, but largely against it. In most free competitive business there is no such inherent antagonism between private and public good.

The privileged monopoly is found not only in the lighting and transportation combinations in cities like New York, Philadelphia, St.Louis, and Chicago: it is in a whole nest of industries--oil, mining, and timber-- which are interknit with our railroad system.

Here is the real antagonism between monopoly and good citizenship. Anthracite coal is not a business apart--it is a railroad business; and if there are abuses, they cannot be corrected apart from railroad regulation. There is nothing that we now need to know so thoroughly as that the railroad is the one key to the control of all monopolies, including those that often last just long enough to gut the properties according to get-rich-quick principles. The waste of the public wealth under this concentrated stimulus is the darkest economic fact, as the ugliest political fact is the corruption of officials and legislators.

Think of a product so vital to the future as the forests; and then picture, if you can, the waste and despoiling of this strictly common wealth that has gone on, and still goes on, in connection with unregulated railroad affiliations,--properties, larger than several Eastern states, stolen, and then burned, and skinned, and devastated, so that two generations cannot repair the loss! And now by highest federal authority we are warned that our timber supply cannot last twenty-five years without a new controlling policy.

Yet it is not, of course, the monopoly that is the evil. It is solely the way in which we have allowed the monopolies to be owned and controlled. We have admitted a kind of irresponsible proprietorship that has so debased political methods in the United States that we are made at the present moment (in this one respect) a warning to the world.

Last year a social investigator returned from New Zealand. He said: "I found their able men chiefly anxious to avoid the example of the United States. Their problem is to develop a rich and prosperous industrial life, but escape the rottenness of American politics. Whether they succeed or fail, their purpose is great." Their plan is to use the strength of the government to prevent the formation of private monopolies such as have debauched our politics until we have become a mockery among the nations.

How long we ourselves have talked of political corruption as if it were separable from the privileged monopolies in business! That we now see this sorry partnership as it is, and are daily more and more aroused by it, and bent on its dissolution, is the surest sign of progress, as it is the surest sign that democracy need not fail.

Again and again we wonder how long it will require for the sovereign people to learn a lesson so simple. How many more facts or revelations do we need?

The other day a liberal theologian told me that he had been preaching some elemental truths about a larger religious life. A sturdy old listener, who knew they were truths, but didn't quite like to adjust himself, said to the preacher: "I guess that's all true that you've been preaching; but--I don't more'n half believe it."

We, too, know these truths about the monopolies; but we still hesitate,--we still act as if we didn't "more'n half believe it." But if the monopoly as such is not an evil,--if the evil is the practice of political abuse by irresponsible private ownership,--what are our alternatives when the question of remedies is raised? Are we forced to the logic of the socialist,--that the city or state should take these monopolies out of the categories of private property, owning and managing them directly for the people? The socialist tells us that these combined interests in transportation--mines, oil, timber, etc.—have become a power with which city and state cannot cope; that we are at the present moment governed by these monopoly interests, and shall continue so to be governed until the state has absolute possession of them.

To this claim of the socialists, one reply is obvious. Every immediate political duty now before us is committed to the principle of regulation. For some years we are going to try that. We are not going to assume that mines, oil, timber, elevators, and our vast transportation system with its connecting monopolies, are all to be taken under state proprietorship and managed as our postal system is now managed. For any future worth discussing, we are going to use our strength to regulate these monopolies in the public interest. In that decade when the people are at last convinced that these monopolies are more powerful than government; that we have no hope of curbing them into obedience before the law,--in that decade the cry will go up for government ownership on a scale far wider than that of railways and telegraphs.

At this point I do not wish to hedge or shuffle. That the younger of my hearers will see far more government and city ownership than we now have, seems to me so obvious that the discussion of it is not even interesting. Our government must have an economic basis strong enough and broad enough to give it footing against all unfair private monopoly. But this degree of government ownership does not land us in Socialism. It may, indeed, protect us from every dangerous excess which Socialism carries with it.

When the German government secures a large mining property with the distinct understanding that, if necessary, it shall be worked in the public interest to break a private coal monopoly, we have an illustration of one step which our own government ought also to take. The object, in this case, is not to go into a new business, but to break monopoly power, actual or threatened. Or consider that brave experiment station, New Zealand! Her Compulsory Arbitration may fail; she may be forced to an industrial pace slower than we like; but the main purpose of her social policy is sound to the core; and we are now trying clumsily to imitate it. Yet we are still afraid--we "don't more'n half believe it." Her purpose is to use the power of city and state in New Zealand to prevent the private fleecing of the people through monopoly. Whether it is her land policy or her insurance policy, the aim is to check at their source inherent monopoly abuses. One is forever hearing that New Zealand is being given over hand and foot to Socialism. The only trouble with the statement is that it is not true. If you tax a vast estate down there so that it must be cut into small holdings upon which some twenty times more people can live than lived on the private estate, and if this added population is encouraged to win more and more interest and profit-bearing forms of wealth, you have a situation in which the thoroughpaced socialists may be entirely out of the game.

The essence of the socialist's logic is, that all interest on money and all profits on goods made for the market (as well as all rent) are inherently vicious and antisocial so long as they drop into private pockets. There is no distinction between the greedy *abuses* of capitalism through organized privilege and the possible _uses_ of capitalism under regulation.

But think of this issue as we may, we are as a fact now committed to regulation--committed to a long and hard struggle to bring monopoly evils under social control. This is now our situation and our problem.

Yet how easy it is to put these evils into phrases! How hard it is to relate ourselves to definite and effective proposals for the elimination of the evils! Such proposals have nevertheless been at last put before us with coherence and with deliberation. They have been put before the American people with a clearness which cannot be shirked without bad faith on our part. They have been brought within the sphere of practical politics, where their decision now waits upon the choice of the people as a whole.

This commanding policy for future as well as for present interests, for the entire people as well as for the few, has been stated in its integrity in two messages from President Roosevelt. Men may differ about the Philippines; about our military and naval ambition; about nature-fakirs and race-suicide; but about the ordered and constructive purpose to curb the abuses of our ill-regulated private monopolies, there should be no disagreement among sane and disinterested men. No one has ever yet shown genius enough to do disagreeable duties agreeably to all men. To the end of time, if we ourselves are inconvenienced, we shall probably say: "Of course this thing ought to be done,--but it should be done in some other way." The various methods of railroad regulation may irritate us, but that the railroad must be brought so far under public control as to obey the law and serve all men with approximate fairness, no human being who is intellectually and morally awake can longer deny.

To begin this great task with the machinery of transportation was the first clear duty. Scarcely one of the gigantic abuses can be touched apart from these highways of distribution. We have but just waked up to the plain stupidity of giving away so recklessly all sorts of franchise grants, and are

155

beginning to see the equal stupidity of parting madly with such an overwhelming part of the main and primary sources of wealth--mines, forests, water-power, oil deposits, and ground areas in large towns. These are the sure nesting-places of monopoly, and therefore, of all the fantastic extremes of wealth which make puppets of our politicians and set before the youth of the nation snobbish and materialistic ideals.

This policy, be it remembered, does not ask, as the socialists do, for all forests, all mines, or all the water-power. It asks that the hand of government control be kept firmly upon such portions of these resources as are susceptible to vicious monopoly. All this is possible along the lines of state regulation, without even raising the question of universal ownership. We have a chief executive who sees what the evils are and dares to face them. Yet the courage involved is not his highest gift; but, rather, the intelligence with which he has so stated and grouped the issues as to give us a coherent administrative policy that works toward equality and not away from it.

To group those sources of monopoly that may still be saved; to show how this retention will fortify the government in its great struggle to regulate privileged capital,--is a service that should command the intellectual and moral sympathy of an entire people. It is a policy broadly public and social, as against any lower and partial interest. It is a policy for the whole and for the many, rather than for the monopoly-coddled few. It is a policy that looks to the future rather than to the possible dividends of the next six months. Not separable from it is the President's proposal to put upon these huge accretions a decent inheritance tax. He does not spoil his case by conventional or academic timidities. He does not ask this tax merely as a fiscal device, but as a measure that makes for more rational, social equalities. He asks it in order that the common wealth may grow larger and the top-heavy fortunes (the larger portion of which privilege has made) may be lessened for the common good. The fatuous outcry that this is to be opposed because it is "Socialism" will, of course, continue, although the most conservative governments in the world have long proclaimed it with such conspicuous success, from the public point of view, that it is no longer questioned.

With jaunty prodigality we have scattered these primary sources of wealth precisely as we scattered transportation and other franchises upon which dangerous private monopolies were built. The kind of mistakes that have been made with the franchises, we have in this generation come to see clearly. In the teeth of extreme difficulties, we are trying to protect the public through legislative control of these corporations. We are learning the same lesson in our forestry. We have the lesson still to learn in remaining mines, oil-lands, water-powers, and phosphate-beds. Nothing in the statesmanship of President Roosevelt will more surely win him laurels in the future than his pluck and consistency in forwarding this policy, which stands for the whole people and for the future. It is as serenely above party as it is above corporate or private interest.

The warring and balancing of sectional, partial, and immediate interests will always have their claims; but the next clearest step in civilization is to learn the political habit of acting also for the social whole. Social politics, so called, already has this character.

The forestry legislation of Switzerland or Germany has its inspiration in the thought for the whole people and for future generations.

Many years ago I heard a discussion in Germany among three art-teachers,-- two of them with a world-wide fame,--that was as new to me as it was amazing. They seemed to agree that the art of the sculptor reached its height in the Age of Phidias; that never again would men give shape to figures fit to be put, let us say, beside the Elgin Marbles. As some nineteen centuries passed by, another art came to its finest flowering in the Italian Cinquecento, when Raphael, Da Vinci, and Michael Angelo added color to form. They agreed that never again would paintings be produced fit to be classed with the Sistine Madonna. Another two centuries passed, and the Bachs began the great music which these three modern artists thought of as the reigning art of our time. Here came their question, "What is to be the next and coming art that shall compare with the Greek period, with the Cinquecento, and with modern music?" One thought it would be the theatre. He wrote, I believe, a pamphlet to prove this. I do not recall the guess of either of the others; but I venture to make my own guess.

Art is knowledge in its applications; and to apply our experience and our knowledge to the shaping of a higher social justice is also an art.

It is an art already showing itself in the field of politics and social reconstruction; a politics, enriched and ennobled by ideals of citizenship, freed at last from that party machinery whose boss has been the puppet of business men fighting for monopoly privilege. It will be a politics not for the few or the favored; not alone for the strong and successful; but a politics for the common weal, for the common and inclusive good of every citizen according to his good will and honest endeavor.

Here is a sphere for art as much nobler than that of sculptor or painter as the destinies of human life and society are higher than those of any inanimate object, even though carved by Phidias or painted by Raphael.

It is, above all, an art that should touch by its inspiration the gallantry of the whole student class. The very breath of it is the shaping and directing of those conditions out of which may emerge a society in which the spirit of justice and equal opportunity will be realized at least so far that it will be no longer a mockery among honest men.

HIGHER EDUCATION AND BUSINESS STANDARDS
BY WILLARD EUGENE HOTCHKISS

Last summer, when we reached California for a year's sojourn, we had the good fortune to secure a house with a splendid garden. A few weeks ago, after the early warm days of a California February had opened up the first blossoms of the season, our little five-year-old discovered that the garden furnished a fine outlet for her enterprise, and she soon produced two gorgeous—I will not say beautiful—bouquets. Barring a certain doubt about her mother's approval, she was well satisfied with her achievement, she felt a sense of completeness in what she had done—and well she might, for she had not left a visible bud.

There is a strong tendency to go at business the way Helen went at the garden. She knew what to do with bouquets; raw material for making them was within her reach; what more natural than to turn it, in the most obvious and simple way, into the product for which it was designed. From her standpoint such a procedure was entirely correct—she was making bouquets for herself and her friends; everyone in her circle would share the benefit of her industry.

Whenever in the past business enterprise has proceeded from a similar viewpoint, we have stood aside and let it proceed; it was not our garden; we were quite willing to take the rôle of disinterested spectators. Recently we have discovered that it is our garden; we have learned that we are not disinterested; we now see that business plays a large part in the life of every one of us. That being the case, we assume the right to question its processes, its underlying policies, and its results. We are gradually coming to think of business in terms of an integrated and unified national life. We desire the national life to be both wholesome and secure.

What the public really wants from business, then, is a contribution to national welfare, and it has become convinced that, by taking thought, it can make the contribution more certain and more uniform than it has been in the past. Many business men share this view; with varying zeal they are trying to work out standards of organization that will insure the kind of regard for general welfare which the public has come to demand.

This is the new idea in business; it has already taken deep root; but it needs to be further developed. We have the difficult task of reducing an idea to a practical working plan. How shall we go about it? Fortunately the idea itself contains a hint for further procedure. A new attitude in business must be coupled with a new attitude in public policy.

When my enterprising child made an onslaught on the garden it would have been easy enough to punish her; but it is doubtful if mere punishment gets very far in a case of that sort. Unless we can teach the child to enjoy the garden without destroying it, the restraining influence of punishment will be no stronger than the memory of its pain or the fear of its repetition. This memory of the past and fear of the future usually wage a most unequal contest with the vivid and alluring temptation of the present.

But should not the child be restrained? As far as necessary to protect the garden, and perhaps also to make her conscious of an authority in the world outside of her own will, yes—but that is not the main task. The main task is to educate her, to develop an understanding of the garden, to get her in the frame of mind in which she will derive her greatest enjoyment when she cultivates it and sees it grow, and when she restricts her picking to a reasonable share of what the garden produces.

In the actual case before us, the child was after quick and easy results, the only kind she could comprehend; she was unable to look upon the garden as a living thing whose life and health must be preserved to-day in order that it may yield returns to-morrow and next week. Analyzed with adult understanding, her essential fault was a failure to get beyond immediate results and to view the garden from a long-time angle. We ought not to expect her to do this now, but we do expect her to do it when she is grown up. We expect in time so to educate her that she will be able to think of the garden in terms of permanence and growth and to make an effective use of it from that standpoint; and this same education in long-time effectiveness is what we want in business.

Business standards must be discussed from the standpoint of efficiency, but efficiency needs to be interpreted. We may as well admit at the start that the efficiency ideal is not entirely in good repute at this moment.[1] If I may import an expression from England, we have been somewhat "fed up" with efficiency during the recent past and the ration has been rather too much for our digestion.

Away back in the eighties, before the dominance of business in American society had been questioned, efficiency, as the term was then understood, had a place among the elect; it was the intimate associate of business success. Then came the muck-raker, and with him came also anti-trust cases and insurance investigations. We turned our attention to labor outbreaks, to graft prosecutions, and to land steals. We talked about "malefactors of great wealth." We even became interested in Schedule K. And so, during the first decade of the new century a whole train of revelations, incidents, and phrases tempered our regard for business and brought many business practices under the ban of law and hostile sentiment. Efficiency was in bad company and suffered in reputation.

But efficiency was able to prove an alibi; we were told that the thing which posed as efficiency was not efficiency, but special privilege, and we were again persuaded of the great service a regenerate and socialized efficiency could render. Just at this point came the outbreak in Europe; efficiency was again caught in bad company, and we began to hear such phrases as the "moral breakdown of efficiency," "efficiency, a false ideal," and others of similar import. In an article bearing the title, "Moral Breakdown of Efficiency," published in the "Century" for June, 1915, it was maintained that pursuit of efficiency had led and was still leading civilization on a downward path.

In addition to the reputation of keeping bad company, efficiency has to bear the odium of many foolish and inefficient deeds performed by its self-appointed prophets. The quest for efficiency has called forth in business a new functionary known as the "efficiency expert." Many of these men have done a vast amount of valuable work, but many others have not. While the real expert has been raising the level of business organization, the others have been piling up a large wastage of poor work and lost confidence.

But these are side issues. The main fact stands out above them. We have been steadily adding to the burdens on industrial and commercial equipment; even more have we increased the stresses and the strains on human life. A devastating war is now suddenly taking up the slack, and the slow and painful task of making the world efficient must be hastened in order that society may bear the load. In these circumstances we need not apologize for making efficiency the main support of business standards. Nor need we assume, as does the author just cited, that the efficiency ideal in any way conflicts with the ideal of moral responsibility and service.

Of course, if we reflect, the abstract and impersonal thing which engineers define as the ratio between energy expended and result obtained has no moral quality in itself. Whatever of morality or lack of morality the word "efficiency" calls forth is given to it by the manner in which the terms of the ratio are defined. It is for society to make the definitions. Society may determine the forms and the limitations under which it will have business energy expended, and it may decide what are the social ends toward which it will have business effort contribute. Guided by wise social policy, efficiency and service go hand in hand.

Since business is subject to control by society, it follows that the efficiency factors in a particular business, in a whole industry, or in business generally, must adjust themselves to the decisions that society has made, and they must also take account of decisions that it may make in the future. And these decisions are not all recorded in the law or even in the vague thing we call public opinion. Laws and opinions of particular groups, group morality, individual morality, even inertia, and a long list of more subtle and often capricious reactions are channels through which social purpose finds expression.

It is worth our while to consider how these reactions may affect practical administration. No reflection is needed to see that in proportion as business men fail to take account of forces outside the business, in that proportion they are likely to miscalculate the results of business policies. Striking examples of such miscalculation are found in the experience of Mr. George M. Pullman back in the nineties, and of Mr. Patterson, of the National Cash Register Company, a decade later. Each of these men, with apparent good faith, undertook to surround his laborers with conditions of physical, mental, and moral uplift, and each undertook to do it as an act of paternal bounty. Each of them, as far as we can judge, expected appreciation, gratitude, and increased efficiency. But they failed to take account of the group consciousness of their laborers; they did not know what the laborers were thinking; and because the laborers were thinking something different from what the employers thought, policies intended to arouse gratitude aroused instead resentment and a strike.

But there are many things besides too much paternalism that may result in a strike. Another concern of international dimensions and one whose officers, I can vouch, are men of high character and public spirit, also found itself confronted with a strike in 1910. This was a highly organized business. For years its sales department had tried to seek out the highest grade of talent, and the result was a selling and distributing organization that was the model and the envy of competitors. But questions of employment seem to have gone by default, the general policy being confined to a sincere but vague good-will toward employees and acceptance of things as they were.

The issues of the strike were issues with which we are all familiar. On the workers' side, grievances and no workable machinery for redress; result: organization, concerted group action, force. On the other side, there was a personal readiness to hear grievances, coupled with insistence on the ancient right of the employer to conduct his own business in his own way, without interference from employees or the public.

After weeks of deadlock the strain of a distressing situation, losses from the interruption of business, regard for public opinion and the opinion of friends, combined with their own desire to do the right thing, induced the employers, probably against their best judgment, to recede from their position. An agreement was made providing for increased wages, standardization of piece-work, a preferential shop, and appointment by the firm of a person to hear grievances and to coöperate with a representative of the union in securing redress.

The union in this case was fortunate in being represented by a high-minded man who was a real statesman. The firm selected a trained economist as labor expert, and he soon had an employment department in operation. Together these men and their colleagues have kept peace in the concern and have developed and expanded the machinery for settling disputes into a model of industrial-relations organization.

Some four years after the strike the business head of the firm testified in a public hearing that he should scarcely know how to conduct his business without the organization which now obtains for dealing collectively with labor. He also in the same hearing expressed the view that a large employer is a trustee of the public, responsible for the measure of public welfare in which his business results; and this man, remember, is not a reformer or even a radical, but just a successful business man.

In this bit of labor history there were, no doubt, many fortunate but uncontrollable factors which, otherwise combined, would have brought a less happy result. But two things stand out: first, the laborers listened to wise counsel—they were well led; and second, the employers, when they consented to make an agreement, gave the plan adopted their genuine support. Combining good citizenship with business sense they were able to understand the new social influences that make the formulas of 1880 a poor gauge of efficiency factors in 1910. They are now enjoying the benefits of their willingness to learn.

The effect of social forces is seen under different circumstances and from an entirely different angle in the present halting policy of American railroads.[2] Here, in addition to other social elements in the question, is the fact of definite government control. This circumstance has accustomed railway managers to look at both the internal and the public factors in their success. A number of years ago, before Mr. Justice Brandeis became a member of the Supreme Court, he pointed out, as many others have since done, that the railroads were looking too much to the government factor, and too little to the economy and effectiveness of their own internal administration. Even though we concede this point, it is still clear that the highest efficiency of our railroads must wait upon a clarification of policy with respect to the great social fact affecting railway operation—the fact of government control. We may not approve the precise manner in which the railroads respond to this fact, but obviously they cannot be efficient and ignore it.

Examples, ranging all the way from accepted and enforceable legal restrictions to the interplay of the most subtle group sentiments, could be multiplied at will to bring out the presence of the social factor in efficiency standards. Were it not that internal business policies, on the one hand, and public policy toward business, on the other, are so frequently vitiated by failure to reckon with the probable reactions which a particular measure will call forth, I should not retard the discussion to emphasize a point so obvious. But though the presence of social factors is obvious, how to measure them is not obvious. General principles that bear on a specific case are hard to locate and difficult to apply. Even the broad lines of social and business policy are not always clear, and the probable trend of future policy is still less clear.

Just what are the principles that are being worked put in order to determine the forms and the limitations under which business energy shall be expended, and how do they differ from those followed a generation ago? Take the other side of the efficiency ratio: toward what results are we trying to have business energy directed? Again, what are the instruments with which society is enforcing its purpose? How effective are they, how effective are they likely to become? Finally, what bearing will this social effectiveness or lack of effectiveness have on standards of business efficiency for the generation about to begin its work?

Even though we cannot answer these questions to-day, we have, to-day, the task of educating the generation that must answer them. More than this, the education we provide for the generation about to begin its work will determine, in no small measure, the kind of answers the future will give. It is, therefore, of great importance that in our ideals and our policies for educating future business men we should try to anticipate the social environment in which these men will do their work.

We are in the habit of speaking of the present as a time of transition—the end of the old and the beginning of the new. In a very real sense every period is a period of transition. Society is always in motion, but that motion at times is accelerated and at other times retarded. Clearly we are living now in a period of acceleration—a period which must be interpreted not so much in terms of where we are, as of whence we came and whither we are going. This means that we cannot hope to prepare an educational chart for the future without understanding the past.

In our study of business we are always emphasizing the "long-time point of view," and we fall back upon this convenient phrase to harmonize many discrepancies between our so-called scientific principles and present facts. On the whole, we are well justified in assuming these long-time harmonies, but it will not do to overlook the fact that many important and legitimate enterprises have to justify themselves from a short-time viewpoint. Of more importance still is the fact that in this country enterprises of the latter sort have predominated in the past. This circumstance has a very marked bearing on the nature of our task, when we try to approach business from the standpoint of education.

There are strong historical and temperamental reasons why nineteenth-century Americans were inclined to take a short-time view of business situations. Our fathers were pioneers, and the pioneer has neither the time, the capital, the information, the social insight, nor the need to build policies for a distant future. The pioneer must support himself from the land; he must get quick results, and he must get them with the material at hand.

Every one of our great industries—steel, oil, textiles, packing, milling, and the rest—has its early story colored with pioneer romance. The same romantic atmosphere gave a setting of lights and shadows to merchandising and finance and most of all to transportation. Whether we view these nineteenth-century activities from the standpoint of private business or of public policy, they bear the same testimony to the pioneer attitude of mind.

Considering our business life in its national aspects, our two greatest enterprises in the nineteenth century were the settlement of the continent and the building-up of a national industry. In both these enterprises we gave the pioneer spirit wide range. With respect to the latter, industrial policy before 1900 was summed up in three items: protective tariff, free immigration, and essential immunity from legal restraints. This is not the place to justify or condemn a policy of *laissez-faire*, or to strike a balance of truth and error in the intricate arguments for protection and free trade; nor need we here trace the industrial or social results of immigration. We need only point out that the policy in general outline illustrates the attitude of the pioneer. The thing desired was obvious; obvious instruments were at hand—immediate means used for immediate ends. From his viewpoint, the question of best means or of ultimate ends did not need to be considered.

In building our railways and settling our lands the pioneer spirit operated still more directly, and in this connection it has produced at the same time its best and its worst results. The problem of transportation and settlement was not hard to analyze; its solution seemed to present no occasion for difficult scientific study or for a long look into the future. The nation had lands, it wanted settlers, it wanted railroads. If half the land in a given strip of territory were offered at a price which would attract settlers, the settlers would insure business for a railroad. The other half of the land, turned over to a railroad company, would give a basis for raising capital to build the line. With a railroad in operation, land would increase in value, the railroad could sell to settlers at an enhanced price and with one stroke recover the cost of building and add new settlers to furnish more business.

In its theory and its broad outline the land-grant policy is not hard to defend. The difficulties came with execution. We know that in actual operation the policy meant reckless speculation and dishonest finance. We know that no distinction in favor of the public was made between ordinary farm lands, forest lands, mineral lands, and power sites. We know that the beneficiaries of land grants were permitted to exchange ordinary lands for lands of exceptional value without any adequate *quid pro quo*; and we know that there were no adequate safeguards against theft.

Wholesale alienation of public property was intended to secure railroads and settlers, but the government did not see to it that the result was actually achieved. Speculation impeded the railways in doing their part of the task, while individuals enriched themselves from the proceeds of grants or withheld the grants from settlement to become the basis of future speculative enterprises. All this seems to show that in execution at least our policy from a national standpoint was short-sighted. Careful analysis and a more painstaking effort to look ahead might have brought more happy results.

And how about the railroads from the standpoint of private enterprise? A railway financier once described a western railway as "a right of way and a streak of rust." The phrase was applicable to many railways. Deterioration and lack of repairs were, of course, responsible for part of the condition it suggests, but much of the fault went back to original construction. It was the wonder and the reproach of European engineers that their so-called reputable American colleagues would risk professional standing on such temporary and flimsy structures as the original American lines. Poor road bed; poor construction; temporary wooden trestles across dangerous spans—everything the opposite of what sound engineering science seemed to demand. Why did not the owners of the roads exercise business foresight to provide for reasonably solid construction?

What seems like an obvious and easy answer to all these questions is that both the Government and the road were controlled in many cases, as the people of California well know, by the same men, and these men were privately interested. As public servants or as officers of corporations they were supposed to be promoting settlement and transportation; as individuals they were promoting their own fortunes. This result was secured by the appropriation of public lands and the conversion of investments which the public lands supported. That this sort of thing occurred on a large scale and that it involved the violation of both public and private trusts is fairly clear.

Public sentiment has judged and condemned the men who in their own interests thus perverted national policy; and we approve the verdict. But it is not so easy to condemn the policy itself or to indict the generation that adopted it. Looking at the matter from the standpoint of the nation, it was precisely the inefficiency and the corruption in government which augmented the theoretical distrust of government and made it unthinkable to the people of the seventies, that the Government should build and operate railways directly. The land-grant policy entailed corruption and waste, of course; but what mattered a few million acres of land! No one had heard of a conservation problem at the close of the Civil War. Resources were limitless; without enterprise, without labor and capital, without transportation they had no value, they were free goods. The great public task of the nineteenth century was to settle the continent and make these resources available for mankind. This task it performed with nineteenth-century methods. From our standpoint they may have been wasteful methods, but they did get results. In its historical setting, the viewpoint from which the task of settlement was approached was not so far wrong.

When we examine the counts against the railroads as private enterprises, we find that the poor construction, which from our point of vantage looks like dangerous, wasteful, hand-to-mouth policy, is only in part explained by the fact of reckless and dishonest finance. I am advised by an eminent and discriminating observer that the distinguished Italian engineer to whom Argentina entrusted the building of its railroad to Patagonia, produced a structure which in engineering excellence is the equal of any in the United States to-day. But the funds are exhausted and the Patagonia railroad is halted one hundred and fifty miles short of its goal; there are no earnings to maintain the investment.

The reaction of high interest rates on the practical sense of American capitalists and engineers has made operation at the earliest possible moment and with the smallest possible investment of capital the very essence of American railway building in new territory. Actual earnings are expected to furnish capital, or a basis for credit, with which to make good early engineering defects. All this, of course, is but another way of saying that the criterion of engineering efficiency is not "perfection," but "good enough." This distinction has placed a large measure of genuine efficiency to the credit of American engineers, and it explains why Americans have done many things that others were unwilling to undertake. It is a great thing to build a fine railroad in Patagonia, but I am sure we all rejoice that the first Pacific railroad did not have its terminus in the Nevada sagebrush. The standard of technical perfection set by the Italian engineer did not fit the facts. It is not the failure to attain his standard but the failure to measure up to a well-considered standard of "good enough" that stands as an indictment against American railway enterprise.

Viewed in historical perspective the business environment of the pioneer appears to have been dominated by two outstanding facts: one, seemingly inexhaustible resources; the other, a set of political and economic doctrines which told him that these resources must be developed by individual initiative and not by the State. The faster the resources were developed the more rapidly the nation became economically independent and economically great, and since they could not be developed by the State it is not strange that private initiative was stimulated by offering men great and immediate rewards. These rewards have encouraged individuals and associations of individuals to aspire to a quick achievement of great economic power, and their aspirations have been realized. Such achievements have been a dominating feature of our business life, and we have regarded them as an index of national greatness.

Abundance of resources, if it did not make this the best way, at least made it an obvious way, for the nineteenth century to solve its business problems. From our vantage point we can see that serious mistakes were made. When we set the foresight of our fathers against our own informed and chastened hindsight their methods appear clumsy and amateurish. But in the main they did solve their problems: they gave us a settled continent; they gave us transportation and diversified industry. We now have our garden and the tools with which to work it. If the pioneer allowed the children to pick flowers and in some cases to run away with the plants and the soil, he did not fail to develop the estate.

Our inheritance from the pioneer is not only material but psychological. The pioneer attitude of mind has made a real contribution to our business standards. The very magnitude of our enterprises, the fact that we have had to develop our methods as we went, our success in approaching problems that way, have given us a confidence in ourselves and a readiness to undertake big things without counting the cost. This readiness is a large, perhaps a dominant, factor in our contribution to world progress. It is not an accident that the greatest problems of mountain railway building have been met and solved by American engineers, or that they have carried a great railroad under two rivers to the heart of our greatest city. These in a private way, and the Panama Canal in a public way, are typical of American engineering enterprise.

As with engineering, so with general business. Our pioneer managers did not lack imagination; they were not afraid to undertake; they were not constrained by worry lest they make mistakes. They made many mistakes. Some were corrected, others ignored, but many more were concealed by an abundant success. The pioneer could afford to do the next thing and let the distant thing take care of itself, and in large measure he escaped the penalties which normally follow a failure to look ahead.

Substantial forces have tended to keep the pioneer spirit alive. If some resources have been depleted, other resources have been found to take their place. Scientific discovery, invention, and the development of technique have placed new forces at our command. Products have been multiplied, but the demand for products has multiplied faster. We have been able to continue offering men great and immediate rewards for the development of new enterprises. As labor was needed, our neighbors have continued to supply it. The result is that our business has continued to go ahead without being too much concerned about the direction in which it was going.

Business has eagerly appropriated the results of science without itself becoming scientific. The difficult way of science makes slow progress against the dazzling rewards of unbridled daring. So many strong but untrained men have been enriched by seizing upon the immediate and obvious circumstance—there has been so little necessity for sparing materials or men and so little penalty for waste—that we have developed a national impatience with the slow and tedious process of finding out.

Along with our technical and business enterprise, with the courage and imagination of which we are justly proud, a too easy success has given us a tendency to drop into a comfortable and optimistic frame of mind. Imagination, intuition, power to picture the future interplay of forces, courage and capacity for quick action—all these qualities are as essential to-day as they ever were to business success. The pioneer environment reacting on our native temperament has given us these qualities in full measure, but it has also given us a habit of doing things in a hit-or-miss fashion. Our very imagination and courage applied to wrong circumstances and in perverted form have often borne the fruit of national defects.

There is a strong inclination to assume that the old approach to problems will bring the same results that it did in the past, and to forget that we are living in a new world. The problems confronting the pioneer were not the problems we face to-day. It requires great ability to draft a prospectus; in many of our greatest enterprises drafting the prospectus has been the crucial task. But a prospectus is not a going concern. There is a vast difference between promotion and administration. In the promotional stage of our business life we were solving problems made up of unknown quantities, problems for which the only angle of approach was found in the formula $x+y=z$. We still have and shall always have problems of the $x+y=z$ type, but if we apply that formula to a problem in which $2+2=4$ we are not likely to get the best results.

Business may not yet be a science, but it is rapidly becoming scientific. Scientific inquiry is all the while carrying new factors from the category of the unknown to that of the known, and by so doing it is setting a new standard of business efficiency. The more brilliant qualities, like courage and imagination, must be coupled with capacity for investigation and analysis, with endless patience in seeking out the twos and the fours and eliminating them from the equation. When it is possible by scientific research to distinguish a right way and a wrong way to do a task, it is not an evidence of courage or imagination but of folly to act on a faulty and imperfect reckoning with the facts.

The person who uses scientific method takes account of all his known forces; he prepares his materials, controls his processes and isolates his factors so as to reveal the bearing of every step in the process upon an ultimate and often a far distant result. In other words, he tries at every stage to build upon a sure foundation. His trained imagination and judgment working on known facts set the limit on what he may expect to find, and interpret what he does find, all along the way.

In so far as particular business enterprises have rested on engineering, chemistry, biology, and other sciences, a scientific method of approach has long had large use in business; but the scientist in business has usually been a salaried expert—a man apart from the management—and it has been his results, and not necessarily his methods, that have influenced business practice. We are now coming to understand that scientific method is the only sure approach to all problems; it is a thing of universal application, and far from being confined to the technical departments of business, where the technical scientists hold sway in their particular specialties, it may have its widest application in working out the problems of management.

The way in which a man trained in scientific method may determine business practice in a scientific manner finds illustration in a multitude of practical business problems, ranging all the way from the simplest office detail to the most far-reaching questions of policy. To cite an example, of the simpler sort: if an item in an order sheet is identical for eight out of ten orders is it better to have a clerk typewrite the eight repetitions along with the two deviations or to use a rubber stamp? Of course, there are not one or two, but many, items in an order sheet and the repetitions and deviations are not the same for all items. In practical application, the rubber-stamp method means a rack of rubber stamps placed in the most advantageous position. It requires also a decision as to the precise percentage of repetitions which makes the stamp advantageous. Then arises the further question, why not have the most numerous repetitions numbered and keyed and thus avoid the necessity of transcribing them at all?

The rule-of-thumb approach to this kind of problem would proceed from speculations concerning the effect of interrupting the process to use the stamp, the result of such interruptions on the accuracy of work, difficulties in the way of necessary physical adjustments, and many other questions that would occur to the practical manager.

The scientific method of approach would first inquire whether there are any principles derived from previous motion study or other investigations, that apply to the case in hand. In accord with such principles it would then proceed, as far as possible, to eliminate neutral or disturbing third factors and to arrange a test. The results of the test would lead, either to a continuance of the old practice, or to the establishment of a new practice for a certain period, after which, if serious difficulties were not revealed, the new practice would be definitely installed.

It should be emphasized at this point, that there is a fundamental difference between investigations or tests which contemplate an immediate modification of practice and those investigations in which research—that is, the discovery of new truths—is the sole object. Tests which are carried on within the business must never lose sight of the fact that a business is a going concern and that it is impracticable and usually undesirable to transform a business into a research laboratory. Scientific methods in business should not be confused with the larger problem of scientific business research. This larger task, if undertaken by the individual business concern, is the work of a separate department. For business generally, it will have to be conducted either by the Government, or by business-research endowments. The point at which, in practical business, research should give place to action is a question that wise counsel and the sound sense of the trained executive must determine.

An example of the contrast between a scientific and a rule-of-thumb approach, as applied to a question of major policy, is found in discussions of the relative advantages of a catalogue and mail-order policy over against a policy of distribution by traveling salesmen. A few years ago the head of one of the largest wholesale organizations in the United States, talking with an intimate friend, expressed fear that his house, which employed salesmen, might be at a dangerous disadvantage with its chief competitor, which did an exclusively mail-order business. The friend comforted him with the assurance that there are many buyers who prefer to be visited by salesmen and to have goods displayed before them. This fact, he held, would always give an adequate basis for the prosperity of a house that employed the salesman method of distribution.

Neither the fear nor the assurance here expressed reveals a scientific attitude of mind. Careful analysis shows, on the one hand, that the mail-order policy is not the most effective means of cultivating intensively a well populated territory. On the other hand, it shows that the expense of sending salesmen to distant points in sparsely populated areas more than absorbs the profits from their sales. Individual concerns have arrived at these conclusions by experiment and accurate cost-keeping and have succeeded in reaching a scientific decision as to which territories should be cultivated by salesmen and which ones should be covered exclusively through advertising and the distribution of catalogues and other literature.

The difficulty that business men find in applying scientific method consistently in the analysis of their problems is strikingly revealed in the labor policy of the great majority of industrial concerns. While many men of scientific training are dealing with problems of employment, probably no concern has undertaken to make a scientific analysis to determine what are the foundations of permanent efficiency of the labor force which they employ. This is not surprising, when we remember how complicated is the problem and how short the time during which we have been emphasizing the human relations as distinguished from the material or mechanistic aspect of business organization.

To state even a simple problem of management, like the one concerning the order sheet, set forth above, is to reveal some of the difficulties of analysis which characterize all subject-matter having to do with human activity. This means that we should not expect results too quickly nor should we be disappointed if the first results of efforts at scientific analysis are not absolutely conclusive. As soon as we recognize that business is primarily a matter of human relations, that it has to do with groups and organizations of human beings, we see that scientific analysis of it cannot proceed in exactly the same way as with units of inanimate matter. The reaction of human relations to changed influences, frequently cannot be predicted until the changes occur. Business, in other words, is a social science and, like all social sciences, must deal primarily with contingent rather than exact data; likewise conclusions drawn from scientific analysis must in large measure be contingent rather than exact.

Although we cannot always isolate our factors, control our processes, and otherwise apply scientific method, with results as conclusive as those obtained in laboratories of chemistry, physics, or biology, we need not therefore reject scientific method in favor of a rule-of-thumb. We should, however, be suspicious of too sweeping claims based on any but the most careful and painstaking analysis of facts by persons who are thoroughly trained in the kind of analysis they undertake.

While a scientific approach will help in solving many problems of business detail, the substitution of scientific method for a rule-of-thumb approach will realize its object most completely in the influences exerted upon fundamental long-time policy, influences which cannot bear fruit in a day or a year. The circumstances of our history have retarded the acceptance of a long-time scientific viewpoint in business, but forces now at work are making powerfully for a scientific approach to business management. First among these is a realization that our resources are measured in finite terms. We have begun to take account of what we have, and we are able in a rough way to figure the loss from what we have squandered. The situation is not desperate, but we can see that it may become so. To insure against possible disaster in the future we need to exercise effective economy in turning resources into finished goods, and we need to eliminate waste in the distribution and the consumption of these goods. In private business the need for such economy is reflected in rising prices for raw materials. In its public aspect we have labeled the problem, conservation.

A second force making for a scientific approach to business is found in the beginnings of a social policy to which I have referred. This policy is showing itself in limitations upon the way in which materials and men may be utilized and in a sharper definition of the business man's obligations to employees, to competitors and consumers. As long as resources are to be had for the asking, while cheap labor can be imported and utilized without restraint, and where no questions are asked in marketing the product, there is not the right incentive to do things in a scientific way. As business becomes more and more the subject of legal definition, as the tendency grows of regarding it as a definite service, performed under definite limitations, and for definite social ends, margins will be narrowed and it will become increasingly necessary to do things in the right way.

The scientific approach to business has made great progress during the past decade. Out of the hostile criticism to which so-called big business has been subjected have come several government investigations and court records, in which policies of different concerns have been explained, criticized, and compared. Besides, business men themselves have become less jealous of trade secrets and have shown an increasing inclination to compare results. A good illustration of this tendency is seen in the growth of "open price associations" and in the spirit in which credit men, sales managers' associations, and other business groups exchange information. In the same spirit, business and trade journals have given a large exposition of individual experience and increasing attention to questions of fundamental importance.

More significant still has been the scientific management propaganda. Mr. Brandeis's dramatic exposition of this movement in the railway rate cases in 1911 at once made it a matter of public interest. Later discussion may not have extended acceptance of scientific management, but it has not caused interest in it to flag. The movement has become essentially a cult. Its prophet, the late Frederick Taylor, by ignoring trade-unionism and labor psychology in the exposition of his doctrines, at once drew down upon them the hostility of organized labor; the movement was branded as another speeding-up device. More serious than the antagonism has been the spirit in which some of the scientific management enthusiasts—not all—

have met it. They seem to assume that their science is absolute and inexorable, that it eliminates disturbing factors and hence needs no adjustment to adapt it to the difficulties met in its application. This air of omniscient dogmatism, together with the disasters of false prophets, has somewhat compromised the movement and has diminished its direct influence. However, business men have been stirred up. They have become accustomed to using the words "science" and "business" in the same sentence. They are in a receptive attitude for ideas. The indirect influence has been great.

A final, and probably in the long-run the most permanent, influence making for the extension of scientific method in business has been the new viewpoint from which universities have been approaching the task of educating men for business. Prior to 1900, university education for business in the few universities that attempted anything of the sort was confined to such branches of applied economics as money and banking, transportation, corporation finance, commercial geography, with accounting and business law to give it a professional flavor. There were also general courses labeled commercial organization and industrial organization, but these were almost entirely descriptive of the general business fabric of the country, and had but the most remote bearing on the internal problems of organization and management which an individual business man has to face. The assumption was that a man who was looking forward to business would probably do well to secure some information about business, but there was little attempt at definite professional training of the kind given to prospective lawyers, physicians, or engineers.

Within the past few years universities have begun to undertake seriously the development of professional training for business. The result has been that through organized research and through investigations by individual teachers and students, the universities are gathering up the threads of different tendencies toward scientific business and are themselves contributing important scientific results. Out of all this there is emerging a body of principles and of tested practice which constitutes an appropriate subject-matter for a professional course of study, and points the way to still further research.

One of the earliest results of an approach to business in an attitude of scientific research, is the discovery that there are certain fundamental principles which are alike for all lines of business, however diverse the subject-matter to which analysis is applied. Substituting the principle of likeness for diversity as the starting-point of business analysis, has far-reaching consequences not only for education and research but for management as well. First among these consequences is the fact that search for elements of likeness leads at once to replacing the trade or industry with the function as the significant unit both of research and organization.

If we start our study of business by separating manufacturing, railroading, merchandising, banking, and the rest, with a large number of more or less logical subdivisions in each field, and then try to work out a body of principles applicable to each subdivision, we soon run into endless combinations and lose all sense of unity in business as a whole. As soon, however, as we approach business from the standpoint of accounting, sales management, employment, executive control, and when we find that lessons in statistics, advertising, moving materials, or executive management, learned in connection with a factory, can be carried over with but slight adaptation to the management of a store, we at once get a manageable body of material on which to work.

Recognition of the principle of likeness and of its corollary, analysis by function rather than by trade, marks perhaps the greatest single step yet taken in the development of scientific business. The principle, however, has its dangers. Analysis by function implies functional specialization in research and a similar tendency in business practice. Without specialization there can be no adequate analysis of any large and complex body of facts. With too intense specialization there is always danger that the assembling and digesting of facts, and especially the conclusions drawn from them, will reflect some peculiar slant of an individual or of a particular specialty.

The accountant does not always go after the same facts as the sales manager, and even with the same facts the two are likely to draw quite different conclusions as to their bearing on a general policy. Specialization, too, may result in setting an intense analysis of one group of facts over against a very superficial view of other facts—or again, an intense analysis of the same facts from one viewpoint with failure to consider them from another, and perhaps equally important, viewpoint. Unless these weaknesses are corrected, the business will lack balance; the work of departments will not harmonize; there will be no fundamental policy; goods sold on a quality basis will be manufactured on a price basis—all of which leads to disastrous results.

Scientific method is the first article in the creed by which business training must be guided. The growing necessity for critical and searching analysis of business problems, justifies all the effort we can put forth to develop plans for training into a structure of which scientific method shall be the corner-stone. But analysis is not all. Following analysis must come synthesis. Somewhere all the facts and conclusions must be assembled and gathered up into a working plan. It is this task of leveling up rough places in the combined work of department specialists, that puts the training and insight of both the executive and the director of research to the most severe test. It is a mark of a well-trained executive that in performing his task he instinctively follows principles instead of trusting alone to momentary intuitions, however valuable and necessary these may be.

And here it is that the second article in the creed of business training appears. The executive's task is primarily to adjust human relations, and the nature of the principles by which these adjustments are made, determines the relations of a concern to its laborers, to competitors, to customers, and to the public. If the executive comes to his task without a mind and spirit trained to an appreciation of human relations, he is not likely so to synthesize the work of his subordinates as to make for either maximum efficiency within the business or its maximum contribution to the life of the State.

The term "executive" in large and highly organized concerns is likely to mean the head of a department. A large proportion of the department heads now in business are men of purely empirical training. Their horizon is likely to be limited and to center too much in the departmental viewpoint. They may perhaps be able to see the whole business, but if they do, they will probably see it exclusively from the inside. There is frequently nothing in their business experience that has made them think of the great forces at work in society at large. As the bulk of business has been organized in the past, there has been no department in which, automatically and in the regular course of business, a view looking outward is brought to bear. If it came at all, it was reflected back from the larger relations and the larger social contacts of the head of the business. Many general executives have been promoted from the position of head of department at a period in life when their habits of thought had become crystallized, and it was not natural that they should entirely change those habits with the change in their responsibilities.

Besides, the economics of competition and a strong group sentiment among business men have tended to make them resist social influences which might react upon the policies of their own business. Superficial conclusions drawn from such experiments as those of Pullman and of Patterson, to which reference has been made, have seemed to justify such resistance and have fortified men in the belief that business and response to social influence should be kept separate in water-tight compartments.

More recently men have been coming to understand the fundamental defects in the Pullman and the original Cash Register plans and have come to realize that even a separate welfare department may be successfully incorporated in a business, if only certain fundamental policies are followed in its management. Still more significant is the view looking-outward and the consequent harmonizing of social and business motives, which is coming in the ordinary development of business policies as a result of their more fundamental analysis.

Perhaps the greatest step toward a fuller consideration of facts on the outside is taken, when a business creates a separate department of employment. It is hard to see how the head of an employment department can have the largest measure of success if he sees only the facts on the inside. A comprehensive application of scientific method to problems of employment leads a long way into analysis of the social facts affecting the people who are employed.

From different angles the same thing is true in other departments of business, notably so in the case of advertising and sales. One of the most obvious outside facts which affect sales, is the location and density of the population, and yet it is a fact which frequently is neglected. Another outside fact, which ultimately advertisers will have to consider, is the consuming power of population. They have been very keen to study our psychological reactions, and in doing this they have undertaken the entire charge of the evolution of our wants. But they have not always gone at their work from the long-time point of view. Sometime they will have to take account of the fact that unwise consumption impairs efficiency and depletes the purchasing power from which advertisers must be paid.

The next step in the scientific analysis of business is to provide for more ample analysis of facts on the outside. Weakness at this point explains the defects in many plans for the welfare of employees, it explains the defects in scientific management, mentioned above, and it explains many other shortcomings in projects for increasing the effectiveness of business.

But men who approach business from the standpoint of university research are not free from the same danger. In their effort to orient themselves with the business facts, they get the business point of view and run the risk of centering attention too much on materials and material forces. Even psychological reactions of men and women may be analyzed from the standpoint of their mechanics, without ever going back to those impelling motives which have their roots in the human instincts and complex social reactions of which the men and women are a part.

Approached from the standpoint of scientific method, the field of conflict between different interests in business and between so-called "good business" and "good ethics" becomes measurably narrowed. I do not mean to give science the sole credit for achievements along this line. More frequently advance in moral standards has been forced on unwilling victims through legislation, public opinion, or class struggle, and then men have discovered, as a happy surprise after the event, that "good ethics" was profitable. But science has done something, and might have done still more, if our efforts at scientific analysis had not been so often underweighted on the human side. These very discoveries of harmony between wholesome practice and good business constitute a part of the body of fact of which a truly scientific method must take account. When a review of all the cases in which compulsion has changed existing methods shows an almost invariable adaptation and a tendency toward better results after the level of competition is raised, a man of scientific training immediately asks the question, whether a fundamental law is not at work.

A glance at social legislation during the last century reveals some interesting uniformities. Every step in the development of the English Factory Acts as they stood at the beginning of the present war, starting with the first Child Labor Bill in 1802 and ending with the Shop Regulation Act of 1912, had been taken against the protest of the most vocal elements in the trades concerned. In nearly every case investigation will show, either that the requirements of the measure enacted fell considerably below the practice of the best concerns, or that the whole industry was in need of some outside impulse to start it in the way of more efficient organization. As long as it is permissible to employ five women and five children to tend five machines, there is not the right incentive to make adjustments by which all five of them can be tended by one man.

In this country in our forty-nine jurisdictions we have been going forty-nine times over the experience of England and other countries, in connection with each effort to force up the competitive level. We have seemed to be quite unable to apply the most obvious lessons of experience either at home or abroad to new cases, and yet essentially the same uniformity of adaptation has occurred here as abroad. Like our employer, whom a strike impelled to adopt an advanced policy toward labor, we find after the event that we should not know how to do business under the standards in force before the law compelled a change.

Enforcement of the Sherman Anti-Trust Law has been frequently cited as an example of unwise government interference. With respect to many of the incidents of enforcements, criticism has been well founded. But the net result of that enforcement has been a much sounder body of law on the important subject of fair and unfair competition. Besides, we now have in the Federal Trade Commission the beginnings of an administrative organization for dealing with the whole subject of monopoly and restraint of trade. And more than all this, we have a better prospect than ever before, of some sort of mutual respect between government and business, and of honest coöperation in working out their mutual problems. It is not likely that the Anti-Trust Law has prevented honest men from earning legitimate profits from legitimate business service to anything like the extent which would be indicated by the vigor with which it has been opposed. But even if it has, we have received something for the price paid.

And so the list might be lengthened, pure food and drugs, meat inspection, public service regulation, industrial safety, and the rest,—in nearly every case, from a purely business point of view, opposition, in so far as it related to the main point of government policy, has been a mistake. Refusal of the business men affected to accept a policy of regulation has tended to shut them out of the councils in making adjustments of detail. This fact has hindered the government in performing a service which in most cases both the public and the business needed to have done.

Even when we admit, as obviously we must, the persistence of conflict between different interests with respect to a large mass of business detail, the fact of group influences and social control still remains an important consideration to which business analysis must give due weight. There has been a large mass of business in this country, in which the community has been unable to recognize any productive service; it has been regarded only as a means of acquisition for those who pursue it. Legislation, public opinion, and the evolution of enforceable standards within particular business groups are tending all the while to narrow the sphere of purely acquisitive business. With respect to that great mass of business which has both an acquisitive and a productive side, these forces are gradually bringing us to an attitude of mind in which we regard gain as a by-product of service.

The public is also recognizing that the purpose of goods and services is to promote individual and community welfare, and as fast as public policy to that end can be worked out, it is carrying emphasis even beyond specific products and services to the social ends for which these products and services exist. In these ways society too is trying, clumsily perhaps, to take a long-time view of its business and to conserve the human values that make for progress.

Obviously it is but a partial and incomplete analysis of a business situation that omits these human factors; a working policy that fails to anticipate their force and then to reduce the zone of conflict to its lowest limits is neglecting an important element in the definition of long-time efficiency. And business men are beginning to see this.

A few weeks ago the manager of a large department store in San Francisco was kind enough to show me his record of departmental profits for a number of months. The fluctuation in relative profits of different departments month by month was apparent, especially the fact that after a certain month several departments which had previously earned high profits became relatively much less profitable. I asked the manager to explain, and he did in this way: At the time when the change occurred a new policy had been inaugurated by which employment of help had been centralized and standardized for the whole concern. As a result, when certain departments which had been decidedly sub-standard with respect to wages were brought up to standard, they were unable to earn anything like the profits which they had previously shown.

Without going into the question of the connection between high wages and profits, of which this incident in my opinion was an exception, it was clear to the manager as to me that the increase in wages in these particular departments had been accompanied by an immediate loss in profits. Furthermore, the manager was unable to determine, from figures available before and after the change, that this loss had been directly compensated by gains in other departments. In order to get his viewpoint concerning the change at issue, I asked him two questions: (1) Why was he willing to make a change of such a fundamental character without being able to ascertain in advance whether or not it would be profitable? (2) In the absence of facts that could be incorporated in the accounts, was it his belief that the change would in time be profitable, and if so, how did he reach his conclusion?

His response to the first question revealed to me an intensely natural but nevertheless complex motive. He said, substantially, that he was confident that standardized employment was the only acceptable policy, from the standpoint of the general manager. Given the necessity of standardizing, it was necessary for the general reputation of the business to standardize upward rather than downward. He wanted his business to be regarded as one in which the best standards of employments obtained. Furthermore, he added, "California will soon have a minimum wage law, and I want this business to be well in advance of any wage standards which may be imposed by law."

Answering the second question more specifically, the manager recognized the advertising value of a reputation for having good conditions of employment. He had discovered no tendency for general profits to diminish or for the rate of increase to be retarded more than temporarily. In the absence of definite facts to the contrary he considered it safe to assume that as soon as the business should become adjusted to the new standards, standardization of wages upward would be profitable for the business as a whole. He wanted to make the change voluntarily and to commence operating successfully on the new basis in advance of competitors.

It is scarcely possible to discuss this sort of business situation with a progressive manager, without feeling that he does not approach business exclusively from the standpoint of gain; in other words, to use the phrase of Adam Smith, he is not exclusively an "economic man." The manager of a modern business, on the contrary, is a man very much like the rest of us, and being such a man he is first of all desirous of conforming to whatever standards are in way of acceptance by that part of society in which he moves. Obviously, these standards are made up of both selfishness and altruism, with selfishness tending all the time to become more enlightened as society advances.

As we come to distinguish more clearly between reward for service and mere one-sided gain, there occurs a parallel change in men's motives; they become more sensitive to social disfavor and to social esteem and less and less willing to devote their lives to activity by which no one but themselves is benefited. In this reaction of altruism with enlightened selfishness there emerges in men's minds a new concept of their own interest and a better understanding of the kind of business policy that in the long-run brings them the greatest reward. Of course, this does not mean that enlightened selfish interest has ceased, or that it will ever cease, to be a motive force in business. But there is a vast difference between selfishness untempered with other motives and selfishness eager for the esteem of one's fellows.

Clearly it is a task of higher education to help promote response to the more enlightened motives. The difficulty which even men of advanced university training have in taking full account of human factors indicates something of the nature and importance of the task. The so-called "scientifically trained" manager tends to undervalue the human factor of his equation. His analysis is likely to be overweighted on the material side. When the university starts—as it is starting and should start—to train future executives, it needs to analyze its own problem, and take full account of the dangers against which it has to guard. Otherwise the training itself will be overweighted on the material side and will perpetuate the weakness that it ought to correct.

The greatest danger in this connection, as I see it, arises out of the distinction between the so-called "cultural" and the "vocational" point of view. This distinction comes to us with a large mass of traditional authority, and we have classified subjects and erected barriers on the assumption that the distinction is real. As far as the training of business executives is concerned, I am confident that the distinction is one which ought never to be made. It is a great misfortune, when young men and women who are preparing for a serious career are permitted to think of culture as a non-functioning ornament; equally unfortunate is it for them to think of their prospective vocations as activities devoid of cultural association.

A few days ago a student who had already selected his profession and was anxious to be about it confided to me, as many others have done, how distasteful he was finding the task of "working off his culture." Does any one really suppose that the sophomore who is "working off his culture" under faculty compulsion, in order to get his college degree, is really absorbing from his study anything which, as the faculty assumes, makes him a better man and yet, as he himself believes, contributes nothing to effectiveness in his profession? Or take the case of the man who devotes himself with professional earnestness to his two, three, or four years of college work—will he find that he has invested his time and his money on a purely ornamental luxury that has no relation to his later work?

The first great element of training which the university can give to future business men is a mastery of scientific method as a means of analyzing problems and synthesizing results. Quite as fundamental as this is the development of an intelligent and sympathetic approach to questions of human relationship. Only the beginning steps in the direction of business efficiency can be taken while attention is confined to the material and mechanistic side of business organization. No secure basis for permanent efficiency can be established until we are prepared to go deeply into the question of human motives and to understand something of the complex reactions that come from individual and group associations. Without such a basis we cannot hope for a nationally effective business organization.

Business is a form of coöperation through which men exercise control over natural forces and thereby produce things with which to satisfy human wants. Any subject well taught, which gives an insight into human relations or into nature and man's control over it, will help prepare a person to deal with the intricate problem of human relations in business—that is, if the student has studied the subject in an attitude of mind to see its bearing on what he is preparing to do.

The question is not so much one of too few or too many so-called culture subjects, but rather of the attitude of mind in which all subjects are undertaken. It is a question of getting such a survey of the great facts of human experience and of so pointing their significance as to enable men to approach a problem of human relationship with sympathy and something of a long-time dynamic viewpoint. When this is accompanied by a mastery of scientific method, the foundations are reasonably secure. Without such foundations, secured either in college or out, analysis of problems in a specialized business field is almost sure to be one-sided and incomplete.

The kind of professional training that I would suggest for the future business executive would be laid on the foundation of a college course of two, three, or four years in which the viewpoint and the varied methods of study in several diverse branches of knowledge had been thoroughly instilled. When the student passed to the professional study of business he would be expected to master the fundamentals of business organization and management, including the basic elements of subjects like accounting, finance, and other divisions of organization common to all lines of business. All of these studies would be pursued with constant reference to the fact that business is carried on in a community in which certain public policies are enforced and in recognition of the fact that business should conform to these policies and help to make them effective in contributing to public welfare.

As the student advances, the course would proceed toward greater and greater specialization, and would finally culminate in an intensive study of some fairly narrow business problem, pursued until the student has mastered it in principle and in detail. The result of his study would be set forth in dignified readable English which an intelligent layman could comprehend and which would make the article acceptable for publication in a journal of standing.

Professional study of business, then, should give students a comprehensive many-sided survey of business and a thorough grasp of scientific method as used in analyzing business facts. It should prepare the student to think complicated business problems through to the end and to put the results of his thinking together into an effective working plan. Finally, it should maintain an atmosphere in which business problems are regarded in a large and public-spirited way.

We are well under way with professional training for business; but if students fail to get the general educational foundation for it, it will not accomplish the best results. If the two, three, or four years of college study is regarded as something purely ornamental and irrelevant, while they are getting it, if it fails to arouse an appreciation both of scientific method and of human values, or if these values are thought of as something to forget when the student comes to the analysis of practical problems, the university will not have done what it might do for the promotion of high standards of efficiency in business.

In all of the discussions I have tried to point out how emphasis in business is gradually shifting from acquisition, to production and service; how there are gradually evolving in business, professional standards of fitness, of conduct, and of motive; and how more and more these standards enter into the measuring of business success. Our educational assumptions still rest too largely on the old dollar standard of success with its well-known inferences about the blood-and-iron equipment with which that success can be attained.

Psychologists tell us that we tend to get what we expect. If we fail to create enthusiasm for the opportunity for service in business; if we assume that young persons who enter business are going to measure their returns in dollars alone; or if we continue to feature, as we have done, the break between the so-called "cultural" and the professional parts of the university course, there will be danger that we shall continue to get the thing for which we plan.

There can be no doubt that many of our old assumptions about the relative dignity and social distinction attaching to different kinds of study, as well as the assumption of a purely mercenary motive in business, have impeded a wholesome reaction between higher education and business standards. These assumptions have created an atmosphere—an objective and subjective attitude of mind, a set of motives and desires, of appreciations and valuations, all of which stand in the way of the most far-reaching educational results.

So far as these assumptions can be rationally explained, they rest on ideas that are in part mistaken, in part exaggerated, and in part obsolete. The application of scientific method to business has created an entirely new relationship between business and education. Scientific analysis and social policy are establishing a new connection between the material and the human facts of business. In the new atmosphere the business executive requires those fine qualities of mind and spirit, and the ability to command these qualities for a given task, which peculiarly it is the work of the university to cultivate.

In proportion as universities have vigorously undertaken this work, and have applied scientific method to their own problem of articulating it with higher education in general, the line of approach to professional business training has become increasingly clear. Among the notable developments of the past decade has been a shifting of emphasis from the training of specialists to the training of business executives. As preparation for executive work comes to be generally recognized as an appropriate field for systematic professional study, the standards that scientific method has already achieved will become fixed and better standards of business efficiency and service will emerge.

ABOUT THE EDITOR

Jack Donahue is a chicken farmer and researcher originally from Jacksonville, Florida.